WITH
A LITTLE
LUCK...

WITH A LITTLE LUCK...

AN AMERICAN ODYSSEY

Helen F. Boehm
with
Nancy Dunnan

Foreword by Letitia Baldrige

RAWSON ASSOCIATES : New York

Library of Congress Cataloging in Publication Data
Boehm, Helen F.
  With a little luck—an American odyssey.
  1. Boehm, Helen F. 2. Entrepreneur—Biography.
3. Porcelain industry—United States. I. Dunnan, Nancy.
II. Title.
HD9611.95.B64A35   1985   338.7′6665′0924 [B]   84-42928
ISBN 0-89256-277-3
ISBN 0-89256-291-9 Limited Edition

Produced by Rapid Transcript
Composition by Folio Graphics Co., Inc.
Manufactured by Fairfield Graphics, Fairfield, Pennsylvania
Designed by Stanley S. Drate/Folio Graphics Co., Inc.

First Edition

Dedicated to Edward Boehm,
my late husband, who was my business partner,
my mentor, and my inspiration. Above all, he
left me a legacy, a great American porcelain
tradition to continue.

"One should give life more than he takes from it."

EDWARD MARSHALL BOEHM
(1913–1969)

Contents

Foreword

When a woman born in Brooklyn of humble parentage has five heads of state concurrently addressing her as "Helen," there *must* be some magic in her life. Perhaps it's a powerful dose of luck, talent, ambition, timing, or chutzpah; perhaps it's a combination of all of those.

Helen Boehm came to the forefront of fame because of her husband, Ed Boehm, a gifted farmer-turned-artist. But she didn't hitch her wagon to a star. She *made* Ed Boehm a star. Quiet and shy, he characteristically shunned the limelight, and if he had not married the woman he did, his beautiful porcelain works of art might never have been recognized. Helen's never-ending stream of energy and imagination catapulted the Boehm name into prominence. She was the first American business-woman invited to mainland China by the Chinese government and also the first woman to buy a polo team and turn it into a world champion team within a year. Helen Boehm simply does not know how to accept the word *no* in business. She has lived her life through a world of yeses.

Her chatty life story is great fun to read. This is no tale of cheap sex and grimy problems. It's a combination of Rebecca of Sunnybrook Farms and Horatio Alger. If I didn't know her so well, I wouldn't believe it, but it's all true. Perhaps growing up in a warm, loving, and protective Italian family gave her the right start in life. But she was also different from the start. She won the junior high school graduation dress design competition, having designed and sewed for her friends at fifty cents a dress. She became the first woman optician in a man's world at Meyrowitz in New York. She was the one Clark Gable came to for his glasses—or was it that she stuck her foot out and, as he started to fall, caught him and put him in the customer's chair? When she and Ed needed the money to start his porcelain studio, only Helen could have managed adjusting a wealthy customer's glasses and, while fiddling with the frame, ask for and *get* the money needed to start the studio.

She was always ready with an idea for Ed, some project to earn him the recognition he sought. When she read that Queen Elizabeth was to make her first state visit to the United States since her coronation, Helen immediately realized that the president would be giving a state gift to the royal pair. Months before her visit was to take place, she had her letter on President Eisenhower's desk, suggesting that since Prince Philip loved polo so much, why didn't the Eisenhowers commission the Boehm studio to make a porcelain statue of the prince in action on his polo pony? (Forget the fact that at this point Ed Boehm had never tackled such a complicated work of art!) When the answer from the White House arrived—yes—Ed Boehm marshalled his forces and produced an intricate, difficult, and beautiful work of art that Helen carried onto the front pages of every newspaper in America, as well as before every television camera between here and Nairobi.

Twenty years later, Helen Boehm was chatting with Lord Mountbatten and learned that the statue of "The Polo Player," now in the queen's sitting room at Buckingham Palace, had left the royal pair "a bit disappointed, because the helmet on the statute is white, while the prince always wears Oxford blue." Helen moved quickly. With the queen's permission, she re-moved the statue from the palace sitting room, changed the helmet from white to blue in her English studio, and then replaced it in the same spot in the palace. How many people other than Helen Boehm are that attentive to customer satisfaction twenty years afterward?

Helen has had a private audience at the Vatican with not just one Pope, but with three, and she has managed to interweave trips to visit top government officials in Saudi Arabia and Egypt, as well as Israel.

This is a woman who really moves! This daughter of Italian immigrants manages to attend royal balls and local New Jersey parish benefits with equal enthusiasm. When the commercial airlines can't handle her precious cargo of Boehm porcelains to the Middle East, she hires her own commercial cargo jet. There's always a straight line between two points; if it's the fastest way she'll take it.

If Helen had not married Ed Boehm, she probably would have gone into the world of marketing and become chairman of one of the world's largest corporations or public relations agencies. There is no one with a better nose for a story. If there's a reporter within ten miles' distance, she finds him or her and gives a good story. As for marketing, she could sell Manhattan Island back to the Indians in fifteen minutes, if someone asked her to. I have never seen anyone who could touch her in the field of promotion.

Helen was out in front of the women's movement for many years without even knowing it. In aggressively marketing her husband's porcelains, she was in an all-male world; yet she remained the traditional *brava moglie Italiana*, a wife in the true sense of the word in caring for her husband. She routinely came home in the evening after hard days on the road, put down her heavy cases of porcelains, and proceeded at once to the kitchen to prepare Ed's dinner (which he often wouldn't eat anyway).

The Helen Boehm autobiography reads like a fairy tale in one sense. I have known her for thirty years and have never stopped wondering at her uncanny sense of timing, her flowing energy, and the great outpouring of love she has for people. It is returned. She is Mother Earth in her bountiful generosity to people and to causes. She has the time to listen to other people's problems. Her own problems, including her continuing difficulties with her eyes, remain her own. She does not complain; she has no time for that in the positive world she inhabits.

When Ed Boehm, the man around whom her world revolved in every sense, died of a heart attack, many thought the Boehm empire would dissolve. They were wrong. Ed Boehm had carefully trained a group of artisans in his craft, which had left him more time in his later years to pursue his love of animals and birds. Helen not only continued the business after his death (with the help of Frank Cosentino, who now holds the business reins of the studio), but she made it stronger and far more successful than before, both here and abroad.

Today she continues to serve as director on several corporate boards, to indulge in her love of horses, and to be hard at work on the next *ten-year plan* for Edward Marshall Boehm, Inc. She starts working on a target of opportunity long before anyone else knows that there is one.

She is always "first," and that is why those of us who have been part of the women's movement all these years admire her. I also love her for her keen sense of humor. She does not take herself seriously.

However, if you plan to do business with her, *you* had better take her seriously! Here's Helen!

—LETITIA BALDRIGE

People—My Energizers

Everyone needs something to spur them on, something to encourage them to do their very best. An actor needs applause, a writer needs inspiration, a dancer needs lights. I need people. People are my energizers.

I can never lecture in an empty hall, but give me an audience of two hundred, two thousand, two million, and I want to make certain that I am projecting and sharing my enthusiasm for my life, my work, my story.

People inspire me to do a good job, force me to stretch. I aim to please beyond the "call of duty." I know no other way. The people I know and admire are from all walks of life, are all colors, are all types. I love them all. Beauty knows no boundaries.

I want to express my special thanks and gratitude to the many people I have met along the way who have guided, encouraged, and aided me in a hundred and one ways.

Without the artists and craftsmen and my staff at the Boehm Studios in the United States and the United Kingdom, these accomplishments would not have been possible.

A special thanks to my attorney and good friend, Judge Harold Coleman, whose dedication to the Boehm firm for the past thirty-four years and what we stand for rises above the relationship of a professional man doing his job.

Dorothy Kay, my alter ego, has been my secretary and right arm for twenty years. She's a part of me and an extension of me; she understands everything I feel, think, and do.

I'm grateful to Nancy Dunnan, who became a good friend while researching and writing this book, and to Letitia Baldrige Hollensteiner, a dear friend and business associate of thirty years, for lending her skillful editing talents and for her contribution of the warm foreword.

My loving gratitude as well to my family for their support; especially Mom to whom I was "Porcelain Queen" from the earliest days.

And my thanks to the collectors and fans who write those inspiring letters challenging me to excel.

It is not possible to mention all those people who offered their friendship and encouragement, who shared their love of the beauty of Boehm through giving to museums, institutions, etc., but I want to express my heartfelt thanks to each and every one of you. You helped make "the Boehm experience" possible.

The Queen and I in the
Winners' Circle

I came very close to missing the final match at Windsor that Sunday, June 6, 1982. Every time I consider the possibility of having missed my polo team's magnificent performance in winning Her Majesty the Queen's Cup, my heart skips a beat or two.

It was a beautiful, sunny day when I left the Connaught Hotel, eager and almost with a joyous skip. This was the big day I had been waiting for; this was going to be an incredible day! The street was filled with cars, taxis, trucks—everything stopped—their motors idling, horns honking, people shouting, no one moving. My limousine was nowhere to be seen. The agitated doorman, trying to calm down several groups of people, was explaining that there was a big demonstration against nuclear warfare going on in the center of the city.

I stood looking at my five suitcases. I had checked out of the hotel and planned on going to the Boehm Studio at Malvern directly from the match to spend several days working with my artisans there on some new porcelain designs.

Leaving my bags behind, I dashed out into the street, running as fast as my narrow skirt would permit. Finally, three blocks from the hotel, I found a taxi, which could only inch forward slowly into the traffic stream. We reached the Connaught front door, the doorman quickly helped me load the bags and parcels into the front and back seats, and we were off, for an arduous hour and a half drive. The bulky suitcases and crates kept sliding around in the back seat; with every fast curve we took, I could feel a new black and blue mark on my anatomy. I wondered if the bags and I would arrive at Windsor Great Park in the same vehicle.

By the time the taxi reached the playing fields, it was covered with dust; so were the driver and I. The meter registered a fortune in pounds, but by now I was so elated we had made it that I would gladly have paid anything. As the driver and I walked with my enormous suitcases toward the official tent, a handsome, erect figure dressed in the uniform of the opposing team strode by on his way to the field to warm up. He waved and smiled, "Hello, Mrs. Boehm." I wished him an absent-minded "Good luck," too excited to take note of who he was. It wasn't until I was settled in my seat, gazing intently at the opposing players, that I realized my well-wisher had been Prince Charles.

The heat was record-breaking for this day of the finals for the Queen's Cup. The humidity was frightful, complained one of the English peers, roasting in his heavy woolen suit. The ground was still rain-sodden, too, so instead of being held on the Number One International Field, the game was played on an adjacent one that was slightly drier, Field Two.

The final game in the round for the cup was between the Boehm Team and Prince Charles's team, Les Diables Bleus (the Blue Devils). There is always an air of genteel camaraderie on British playing fields, but today there was also a strong feeling of tension. An American-sponsored team was challenging the British. Guy Wildenstein of Les Diables had told me when we chatted two weeks before that he found it very difficult to believe that a skilled British team could lose to a newly formed American-sponsored one. (His attitude was typical of what most people at the Windsor Polo Grounds felt that day.) When Guy said good-bye to me after that conversation, he said, "Helen, I only hope you and I both make it to the finals." He had no doubt his team would make it, but he wasn't so sure about mine.

It's true that my team had only been organized a few months earlier. Historically, a team without many months of intense practice together should look sloppy and disorganized. Lord Patrick Beresford had stepped in to manage the team, however, and he did so with such enormous skill that I only wish I could have cloned him to have him manage some aspects of my business!

Just when we thought we had accomplished a miracle in pulling our men and horses into a smooth, unified group, the Falklands crisis occurred, and we had to excuse Eduardo Moore and Tolo Ocampo, both Argentinians and expert players, from our lineup. My only consolation from this crushing turn of events was that other teams suffered equal losses of their Argentinian players. Fortunately, Howard Hipwood from England, twice winner of the Polo World Cup for the Boehm Palm Beach teams, and Stuart McKenzie from New Zealand stepped in to save our Boehm Team.

We didn't need much saving. As early as the second chukka, despite gallant defensive maneuvers by Prince Charles, my team led by a startling 6 to 1. By the time "treading-in time" was called, the score was 7 to 3. (Treading-in time is a gentle custom in which all of the spectators crowd on the field at midgame to step on and replace the loose grass divots that have been scooped up by the ponies' hooves and the players' mallets. The English use the period as though it were teatime; they chat sociably while quietly stamping around the ground.)

Several times during the play I glanced over at Her Majesty Queen Elizabeth and Princess Diana, politely rooting in a most royal, understated way for the Prince of Wales and his Les Diables team. They looked slightly dejected as Major Ferguson, deputy chairman of the Guards Polo Club, sent an aide to lead me to the Winners' Circle. This was the first time I had been presented to Her Majesty, and as I waited for her to speak, I wondered if anyone else around me noticed my nervousness. That was *my* American flag up there, snapping in the bright blue English sky, alongside the Union Jack. I clasped my hands tightly, feigning composure. What a great flash of color those American stars and stripes made in the English sky!

The queen stood facing me now. There were five thousand excited, smiling polo fans pressing close to the royal viewing box on the Windsor Great Park Polo Grounds. She had come but a few steps from Windsor Castle for this afternoon ceremony. I had come four thousand miles for it.

The sun felt hotter every minute on my bare head. I suddenly thought back on all the hats I had purchased but seldom worn in my lifetime. Now when I really needed one, I was bareheaded. The creamy peach complexion of the queen and of many of the women standing around us was well protected under broad hats that, viewed en masse, looked like a colorful garden of straw flowers bobbing up and down on the velvet green lawns of the park. The queen was a tiny figure in her silk print dress of robin's egg blue. She turned to the left toward me and in a soft, beautiful voice said, "*Fine* game. Well played. Congratulations!" Then she presented the cup to Lord Patrick Beresford, for according to custom it is the manager of the winning team who receives the cup directly from the queen. Lord Beresford bowed reverently to his sovereign, with that ease and graciousness with which the English seem to be born, and in his turn presented me with the most coveted of all polo trophies, *Her Majesty the Queen's Cup*. What a day for the Boehm Team!

For the first time since its inception twenty-three years before, the Queen's Cup was leaving Great Britain to go home with a girl from Brooklyn. The victory tasted very sweet. The spectators crowded around the players and me, wildly cheering us. I kissed each one of the players—the manager, Lord Patrick Beresford; the number two, Stuart McKenzie; the number three, Captain Howard Hipwood; and the back, The Honorable Mark Vesty. I could feel the sweat through their jerseys. Their faces were dirt-streaked, flushed from exercise in the sun and in triumph at the win.

This day was the culmination of a grueling two-week tournament involving two hundred specially trained ponies and thirty-two polo players. Throughout every game I had sat and cheered on my players, a one-woman, nonstop cheering team, which obviously surprised the restrained English spectators around me. By tradition, they do not show their emotions on playing fields.

Her Majesty was watching me intently. The silver cup was not attached to its base, and for a moment I felt panicky. "If this cup falls right here on the grass at Windsor just when I'm to curtsy to the queen, I'll die!" But the reliable "little angel on my shoulder" stayed with me. I gripped the silver cup tightly, lowered my eyes, and went into as deep a curtsy as I could muster. How Mama and everyone in Brooklyn would love this—Helen in a deep curtsy to the queen of England in Windsor Great Park. Mama had told me so many times, "You must always do your best, Helen, always your finest. Nothing less." Today my team had done its best and its finest. We had won.

"Your Majesty," I said in such a soft voice she had to strain to hear, "I shall always treasure this handsome cup. It is indeed an honor for my players and for me. We accept it with humility. Thank you."

The overwhelming victory of 11 to 6 had surprised everyone that day, because both teams were evenly matched with handicaps of 22. The British newspapers headlined the story the next day with "British Breakthrough for Mrs. Boehm." *Country Life* headlined its coverage, "The Boehm Team Supreme."

A few weeks after winning the Queen's Cup at Windsor, the Boehm Team won another important one, the seventy-one-year-old Cowdray Challenge Cup. I was on a very tight schedule and had to fly from London by helicopter in order to see it. The game was scheduled to start at 3 P.M. Since we did not know where to land at Cowdray, I made a date with player Mark Vesty, who was also proceeding to the field by helicopter, to follow him to the proper landing site. The pilots of our two helicopters rendezvoused in the air at 2:48 P.M., exactly twelve minutes before the game was to start. My helicopter followed Mark's down, and we both made it just in time.

Immediately after the game my chopper flew me to my studio at Malvern. Since there was no airport, my director, Keith Bufton, had asked our neighbor, Mr. Bishop, a farmer, if we could use one of his fields for landing. It was all set, but we had a tense time when we couldn't find our field marker—a king-sized white percale bedsheet. Finally we spotted it. As Keith Bufton described it, "Helen Boehm emerged from the helicopter, stepping daintily onto the sheet, clutching an enormous cup in her hands. Noticing my rather stupefied expression, she laughed, 'Keith, why so surprised? Doesn't every studio boss show up at work in this manner?' "

My winning team won its fifth cup for the year that day at

Cowdray. Never before in the seventy-one-year history of the cup had it left England. That year I managed to take home England's five most prestigious polo trophies—Her Majesty the Queen's Cup, the Cowdray Challenge Cup, the King Constantine Cup, the Jack Gannon Crystal Cup, and the Phillips & Drew Cup.

I grew up in Brooklyn, about as far away from the Westbury, Long Island, polo set as you can get. That day I left Westbury as far behind as Brooklyn!

2

The Franzolins Made It

Among the thousands of immigrants who arrived on the American shores in 1911 were Pietro and Francesca Franzolin, my parents. They had sailed from Genoa and debarked from a crowded ship at Ellis Island, each carrying a young child, my older brother and sister.

Like many immigrants, they never forgot the exhausting and intimidating experience of entering this promising, brash, new country of America. In the early twentieth century, Ellis Island was a strange and baffling place, teeming with thousands of Europeans, most of them desperately poor and each one frantically hoping to begin a new life in America.

Papa guided Mama and the two children through the maze of endless lines, being pushed as they went by the restless crowds. They heard cacophonous and unfamiliar sounds—German, Irish, Russian, Hungarian, and Yiddish. Like the majority of their fellow immigrants, the Franzolins could not understand the directions shouted at them by immigration officials, for neither knew English. Yet the family was together, strong, in good health, and determined to succeed, even if success in those days meant merely surviving.

Papa straightened his tired shoulders and put his arm around his wife and children—Lewis, his first born, and Michaela, his

7

daughter—and said, *"Finalmente possiamo dire—la terra di Dio!"* ("Finally we can say we're in God's country!")

When the immigration clerk stamped the final document with the United States seal and returned their papers, the Franzolin family was free to leave Ellis Island.

They were at last in God's country. America was the land they had both dreamed of—she while growing up in Palermo, Sicily, and he while growing up in Florence.

How much I admire my parents today. I wonder if I ever would have had the courage to go to a strange place with no knowledge of its language or culture and no family to assist me.

The four Franzolins settled happily in Brooklyn and began the task of planting roots in their new homeland. Years later, my father told us that without his loving, supportive wife and his own talented hands, the family would not have survived. While others around him were unemployed, he quickly found a position as a cabinetmaker for Nann's in Brooklyn. There his skill turned the most uninteresting pieces of wood into handsome pieces of furniture. There is no doubt but that as his youngest daughter I owe my love and feeling for design to the hours I spent watching my father finish small pieces of furniture in our home.

I was next to the last of the five children born to my parents in the house in Brooklyn. First came Anthony, then Mary, Joseph, me, and finally Vittorio. My parents called me "Camalida," a nickname of endearment, and the name stuck with me until I left my mother and our home.

Our clapboard house on Eighty-fifth Street in the Bensonhurst section of Brooklyn was a mansion of a house to me, because I never knew anything different. Today, whenever I see a similar house, I think of it as a tiny little place. But to Camalida growing up in Bensonhurst, home was a palace and a happy one, too.

Our childhood was marred by a tragedy from which my mother never recovered. Vittorio, two years younger than I, was killed by a truck while playing softball in the street. We grieved long and hard, but as a family we had the strongest support system in the world. I remember those days of tears and priests and people and praying and darkness in the house. My mother called us *"i miei gioielli"* ("my jewels"). Except for her thick gold wedding band, we were her only jewels, and after Vittorio's death, we were even more important to her.

Northern and southern Italy were joined in the union of my parents; the hearty, solid, Sicilian blood of my mother combined with the elegant, artistic Florentine blood of my father. Both firmly believed in the traditional Italian ways and wanted us to continue to love and respect the old customs. Italian was always spoken at the table as well as in all day-to-day conversation. Because of my father's wish, we studied Italian at school as our second language. The Franzolin daughters were carefully trained in the domestic arts—sewing, cooking, and managing the household—in preparation for what was assumed to be our role in life: wife and mother. Each day after we finished our studies, we would help Mama prepare the family meal. Since I was the youngest, my job was setting the places at the big old mahogany dinner table. Mama was adamant that it be done properly, with all of the glasses and silverware in their proper places and with everyone's table manners shining as brightly as the crystal. (Years after I was to dine in the houses of people of wealth and old family names, but I never felt at a loss in their company, because my mother was a meticulous teacher of manners.)

Dinner was a family affair that no one was ever to miss. We were never allowed to eat or stay over at anyone's house, and slumber parties did not exist in our neighborhood. We chafed somewhat under the very strict attitudes of our immigrant parents, particularly the girls. My sisters and I were never permitted to walk alone, even to and from school; we were not allowed out after dark unless we were chaperoned by one of our brothers. My repeated remonstrations with my mother were totally ignored. I thought I would eventually be given more freedom, particularly once my sisters were married and out of the home, but such was not the case. Mama appointed herself my chaperone, a position she conscientiously filled right up until the day I was married!

Once in a while, if Mama was busy, I managed to walk home from school with a boy, my heart trembling with the utter excitement of being alone with him. But two blocks from my home, he would give me back my books, and I would continue my walk on the opposite side of the street. In this way, I would arrive home *sola,* as my mother would expect.

I was certain of one thing—that I was the only girl of my age in the entire world who was so strictly brought up. My irritation at this was offset somewhat by my love of school and my pleasure in designing and sewing my own dresses. My earliest academic accomplishments were in the direction of mathematics and bookkeeping, a talent I was to use later in my adult life in helping Ed Boehm build his business.

Papa enjoyed watching me do my homework, especially when I was working on my essays for Italian class. I always got better marks on the essays with which he helped me, and I fear the teacher knew exactly why those marks were better.

He used to tell me wonderful Italian children's stories and help me interpret them into essays that I would write myself. I learned so much from those hours of study with him. There was a boy in my class with a very long nose, and we children all used to make fun of him. After Papa and I read Pinocchio together, I felt compassion for my classmate, who had suffered more than we imagined because of our thoughtlessness. I helped make the rest of the class stop teasing him.

Papa became the proud owner of a seven-passenger Willys Knight, a sleek sedan with a soft canvas top and snap-on shields for windy and cold weather. The ownership of a car was certainly a monumental event in all our lives. The family outings every Sunday afternoon, complete with Mama's delicious picnic lunch, are cherished memories of all of the Franzolins.

Michaela, my oldest sister, absolutely astonished the whole family by getting her driver's license when she turned eighteen. She became the center of attention in the neighborhood on Sundays, maneuvering the big black car through the narrow streets of Brooklyn and out to the grassy fields of Long Island. Michaela was really the big boss in the driver's seat on those Sunday drives, and we were all proud of her. My six-foot-three-inch-tall father turned out to be the worst of back seat drivers, even though he sat in the front seat next to Michaela.

He'd shout to her, "Turn left, Michaela, left!" following that with a cascade of unwelcome further directions:

"Slow down!"

"Be careful!"

"All my *family's* in this car!"

We children, of course, wanted Michaela to drive faster, because we knew what awaited us in the trunk—Mama's special Sunday picnic food. We wanted to reach our destination quickly so that we could dive into the homemade meatballs, bracciolette, provolone, Genoa salami, huge ripe tomatoes, stuffed artichokes, and Sicilian bread with sesame, all usually topped off with Italian figs, prickly pears, and fennel. Mama was very particular about her food; much of it was imported by a cousin in the food business, and the remainder she purchased fresh from the local Italian greengrocer. Papa usually brought along a jug of red wine, often homemade, because "it is good for the digestion." (It was also very strong!)

After devouring the lunch, the boys played bocci while we girls walked in the woods, secretly hoping to run into boys our age. Papa and Mama usually sat up against a tree trunk, resting in the shade, Papa reading *Il Progresso* and the *Brooklyn Eagle*.

The outing to Long Island consumed most of the day; driving was slow because the roads were bumpy and muddy. It was long before Robert Moses installed his highway system. Yet we always managed to reach home before sunset.

We never traveled in the dark, because something might happen to the headlights. Mama always planned on the worst happening. Papa said even something bad happening would be better than the worst happening!

Our trips to Long Island were always well organized and full of adventure. As far as we were concerned, we were on a trip abroad to our own private little country.

One day in the winter of 1933, this wonderfully happy and secure home life came to an end. I got home from school on a February afternoon to find my family sitting solemnly in the living room. I knew something was amiss the minute I saw their faces. Our family physician, Dr. Morvillo, walked right in behind me, his black bag in one hand, his walking cane in the other. I realized suddenly, upon seeing him, that the person missing from the room, my father, must be very ill. Papa had not been feeling well at all lately.

Mama followed the doctor upstairs, and Michaela moved all of us children into the kitchen. I had a chance later to peek into Mama and Papa's bedroom. The dark brocade curtains were drawn, and it looked gloomy and forbidding. I saw Papa lying very still in the big mahogany bed, his eyes closed. I was suddenly very frightened, for I had never seen my big, strong, and mighty Papa look so pale and lifeless.

The wait in the kitchen seemed endless. We sat on chairs, no one speaking. Even Mary, the most talkative of us, was uncharacteristically subdued. When the doctor came in to talk to us, we could all tell from the look on his face that the news was very, very bad.

Two days later, we lost Papa. I was thirteen years old.

The Sicilian Sewing Machine

In 1934, a year after Papa's death, I entered New Utrecht Junior High School in Brooklyn. I still deeply missed my wonderful Papa's laughter and love. Fortunately, Mama, who was far stronger than her tiny five feet two inches suggested, gave me the support and attention I needed, even though she was now working full-time at home embroidering linen to support the family.

All of us children took odd jobs to help out. It was a time of great family togetherness and warmth. My brothers automatically assumed Papa's position as head of the family, so it was as though I now had three fathers to replace the one I had lost. As a triumvirate, they were united in protecting me, their little sister. Many times I longed for greater freedom, but as an unmarried Italian daughter, I was not permitted independence, at least in actions. I had plenty to say to my brothers on the subject of their strictness. Their answer was "Wait until you're married, when you're *sposata*."

When I turned fifteen, I was given permission to attend my first boy-girl school dance. On a wintry Saturday morning, with Mama and my sisters in tow, I journeyed to the fabric department of Abraham & Straus to purchase material for my dress. I can still see the four of us chattering gaily over the endless bolts of silk, peau de soie, and vivid taffeta. After much discussion

13

and mock despair, I settled on a white and red polka dot voile with a yard of red velvet for the sash.

For weeks, in the evenings after my homework was put away, I bent over Mama's sewing machine, determined to gather the ruffles perfectly on my first grown-up party dress. Mama patiently showed me how, insisting that I rip out and redo the seams until the dress was expertly finished. One learns great lessons when one is young, and Mama's philosophy was that perfection is the only thing to strive for—and perfection, as she showed me, requires perseverance.

She made me understand the importance of the smallest detail. I remember so clearly sitting with her on the brown and beige hooked rug in the living room, cutting our dresses from various fabrics through the years. She was a true perfectionist.

On the day of the junior high school dance, I was so excited I couldn't eat. I hadn't slept one minute the night before. I kept running to the mirror, exclaiming over what I thought was a giant rash. It was nothing but the flush of excitement. Mama failed in tempting me with my favorite veal parmigiana at supper, and I watched impatiently as she carefully pressed my beautiful new voile full-skirted dress with its starched petticoat. She helped me dress, fastening the tiny row of buttons up the back and tying my red velvet sash. Catching sight of myself in the long mirror, I smoothed my skirt and decided I looked tall but rather nice! Even my brothers noticed that their skinny sister had suddenly blossomed into a young woman.

A girl friend and I walked to the dance together, giggling and delaying all the way so that we would not be too early. We joined a cluster of nervous, twittery girls from our class, enviously eyeing friends who already had partners. But soon I was dancing, too, with a tall, gawky boy from my algebra class. I said a little prayer that he would ask to walk me home. (How times have changed. Today, I would ask to walk him home!) Of course he never had a chance. My brothers Joseph and Anthony suddenly appeared in the middle of the gym on their humiliating mission to collect their little sister and take her home. My dancing partner was truly bewildered. He had never known a girl who had to be home from a school party by 9:30, especially one who was fetched a half hour earlier!

I was mighty embarrassed by my brothers' arrival to take me home, but I also realized that they were merely carrying out a promise made to Papa before he died. I knew that one day this overly protective pattern would end and that I would be free to discover the outside world.

Meanwhile I had a new interest, fashion design. Many of the older girls noticed the clothes I had designed and made for myself. They asked me about them, and when I told them how I made them, they begged me to sew for them. And so, at the age of fifteen, I launched my first business enterprise, charging fifty cents per dress and occasionally seventy-five cents if it was a complicated ensemble. These clothes became the end result of my imagination.

I was commissioned by a girl friend to do a costume for a masquerade party, and I had great fun because I designed something that I would have loved to wear myself. I made a pirate dress of rather intricate design for my friend, with many layers of black net. It took hours of work to get it just right. To me this sort of thing was a magnificent hobby for a girl.

I marketed my ideas by telling my friends about the dresses I would like to make for them. I knew what they wanted, and I also knew what *I* wanted. The combination was a product that was very salable. In this way, I earned some spending money, because there was none in our little bank at home. Mama used every cent to run the house and to keep us fed. Sewing became my first successful career, but I never dreamed as I sat there cutting and sewing that I would one day head a major international company.

The culmination of my sewing career came with a dress that I made for graduation from junior high school. We were supposed to make our own dresses in our sewing class. My design, a white organdy sashed dress with a double-flounced cape collar and a three-tiered ruffled skirt, won first place in the competition against ninety other girls. My teacher assumed that I had used a *Vogue* pattern because the dress was so sophisticated and complicated in its design. I never let on that I had designed the dress myself or that I had never used a pattern for any of my dresses. After all, a *Vogue* pattern in those days cost seventy-five cents, and I did not have seventy-five cents. Necessity is the mother of invention, and I became a darn good pattern maker. My eye enabled me to design, cut, and fit without benefit of a pattern. No one can understand the pride I felt when I walked up to receive my prize for having made the winning dress. I was number one dress designer at graduation, and I told Mama afterward that I was going to try to be number one always in all my endeavors.

To this day, when I am being fitted in haute couture salons in Paris or Rome, I am very fussy with the fitter because I know perfectly well his or her *métier*.

Shortly after graduation from New Utrecht High School in 1938, my mother made an appointment for my annual eye checkup with Dr. Nathan Gillis, the family optometrist. His office was located on the corner of Bedford and DeKalb avenues in an impressive turn-of-the-century building. I had always loved going to his office; it was like taking a long journey. I felt important, and besides, I loved all the equipment the doctor had. As a child, it had always been fun poking around his instruments and playing at giving my doll an eye examination. It had fascinated me to open a drawer and find all those artificial eyes staring at me. Although I was a high school graduate at this point, my mother still chaperoned me, even to the optometrist's office.

On this trip I overheard my mother say, "Please, Dr. Gillis, wouldn't you have a position in your office for a smart girl like my Helen?" Mama did not mince words.

Dr. Gillis was a robust but scholarly looking man. You'd have thought he was a classics professor at Oxford or Cambridge rather than an examiner of eyes and a grinder of lenses in a Brooklyn laboratory. I was furious at my mother for putting him on the spot about a job without having mentioned it to me first.

Then I realized Mama must have thought about this long and hard. She was head of a family that had to be supported and whose members had to learn to take care of themselves individually, too. When Dr. Gillis replied he spoke in a kind voice. "Well, yes. Actually I do need a receptionist, since the woman who is here now is getting married. Would you like to be my receptionist, Helen?"

If there had not been an opthalmoscope in the way, I would

have leaned over and kissed this wonderful man. He was giving me my first break. I was now employed!

Within a week Mama and I were traveling daily to and from Dr. Gillis's office. I protested that I was the only girl in New York who had to go to and from her job in the care of her mother. I wore a white uniform and white shoes, which were a chore every night to keep spotlessly clean. I was proud of my job and my new status in life because I felt like a professional. There was only one obstacle left to hurdle—my mother and her chaperonage. I simply had to convince her that I was a big girl now and could take care of myself. Mama finally agreed, although reluctantly, and she said a rosary every time I was in transit. That meant a lot of rosaries, but suddenly for the first time in my life, I felt free.

Mama and I Meet Ed Boehm

There was only one good thing about World War II, as far as I was concerned. It brought me a husband.

My brother Anthony was stationed at the Air Force Convalescent Center in Pawling, New York, while he was recovering from pneumonia. Mama and I took the train up and back nearly every weekend to visit him during the months he was recuperating.

After the third visit, I noticed a handsome man with thick black hair and a moustache talking and laughing with the injured soldiers in the Rehabilitation Center. This was the section of the hospital where the wounded were trained to use their hands again through woodworking, sculpting, leather tooling, and other crafts. The striking-looking man had his hands full of wet clay and was showing the men how to model figures. I had to find out who he was. There was something special about him.

I looked around and found no one who could introduce us. I was not to be deterred and took matters into my own hands. I boldly approached his work table.

"Are you the instructor?" I felt that if he said yes, I would sign up for his course on the spot, even though I couldn't have cared less about clay modeling.

"Certainly not. The canine and farm animal rehabilitation program is my project."

"What's your name?" I asked, feeling increasingly aggressive.

"Ed Boehm," he replied, but he didn't ask me my name, as I hoped he would. Instead he began talking about his work as a member of the special animal husbandry division of the air force. He was teaching wounded soldiers the care and feeding of cattle, dogs, and other animals as well as how to prepare them for shows. He told me how animals could make despondent soldiers regain their love for life. Patients often left the center at Pawling with a devoted pet at their side. I was fascinated. In his spare time he experimented with clay sculpting. He was modeling a Percheron mare and foal while we talked. I watched him with awe, for he worked with such deftness and skill. His hands, busy creating a work of art, were like a surgeon's. I was spellbound, and for one of the few times in my life also speechless. I instinctively knew I was going to marry this man. The fact that he didn't even know my name was inconsequential.

On my next visit to the hospital I wore an outfit I had designed and made myself at home; a flower-patterned skirt and white organdy blouse with a high ruffled collar. Mass was scheduled for ten in the morning and I was early. I was sitting in the lobby of the convalescent center when Ed walked over and sat down next to me. He was dressed in spotless pressed khakis and a necktie.

"I see you're visiting again. Is your husband or boyfriend here?"

"I'm here to see my brother. And my name is Helen . . . Helen Franzolin." I could feel my heart pounding as I glanced at my watch.

"Do you have an appointment?"

"I'm going to ten o'clock mass."

"Fine. So am I. I'll walk over with you."

So we walked together to the hospital chapel and attended mass. I was impressed with the fervent manner in which Ed said his prayers—so seriously, with great devotion and half out loud.

Then toward the end of the mass I heard several unfamiliar words. As I listened more closely, he whispered with a smile, "I'm a Baptist, not a Catholic. I thought if I told you that, you wouldn't let me come with you."

That was our first "date." I was twenty-four; he was thirty-one. Little did he know that three months later we would be married, thanks to some deft Franzolin maneuverings. As Ed accompanied me to the door of my brother's room, I was already secretly planning our second date. I would invite him out to dinner on my next visit to the hospital.

As in everything else in my life, our courtship was not a usual one. Mama went on all of our dates. You would have thought I was a nineteenth-century sheltered child, or at least the daughter of a South American diplomat. There is no question that my mother, Ed Boehm, and I made a very unlikely trio, dating in Pawling, New York. Soon we were recognized wherever we went. We had dinner at the local inn, lunch in the big mess hall, and we walked about the hospital grounds. For fifteen minutes on each date, Ed and I would manage to sneak away and be by ourselves. Usually it was when Mama was in the ladies' room. I figured out that if Ed could do as well in our marriage as he did in those fifteen minutes every Sunday, then this would be a good marriage.

One Sunday afternoon, Ed took me into a big barn where there were many cows lined up in their stanchions. He pulled a tiny wooden stool up next to a large cow that had been groomed for a local dairy show. It was a Guernsey, Ed said admiringly, but to his displeasure, at that time the name meant nothing to me. All cows looked alike to me. To Ed, they were precious creatures of God. But this was the first cow I'd ever seen up close, and I would just as soon have not been that close. I was quite frightened by the animal, though I tried not to let on. Ed, totally unaware of my discomfort, began milking the cow, telling me exactly how it was done, as though I should be fascinated. All of a sudden, I felt warm moisture dripping down my arms and legs. Ed had sprayed milk straight from that Guernsey cow all over my best silk dress.

"Ed Boehm!" I shouted. "You're absolutely outrageous! What kind of a Sunday date is this?"

As you can imagine, I had a hard time explaining my soiled dress to my mother. From then on, she kept even closer watch over us.

Then finally Mama invited Ed to spend a weekend with us in Brooklyn. All three of my brothers were away in the service, which meant that Ed could sleep in one of their bedrooms.

That really was a first for our family. My sisters had never been allowed to have their boyfriends sleep over, but my mother knew Ed well by now, and that made all the difference. She was comfortable with him, and the fact that my brothers were away gave me a little additional freedom. There was, however, no question of any shenanigans going on in anyone's bedroom. In those days, you knew what you could do and what you could not do, and no one would have dreamed of misbehaving in Mama's house (even, as one of my brothers once said, "if Mama was three thousand miles away").

Mama very quickly came to share my affection for this man who thought milking cows and modeling animals were part of the finer things in life. Ed introduced Mama to a world that was entirely new to her, and she began to admire him as much as I did. She felt great empathy for him, too. His parents had separated before he was born. His mother died when he was only seven, and his entire childhood from then on was spent in a Maryland orphanage. It was there that Ed had found consolation in the farm animals. He worked helping care for the animals, and he milked the cows for the children's breakfast. This kind of work interested him far more than the books he was supposed to study.

When he was sixteen, he left the school to find farm work, but he knew that he needed more formal training in order to get ahead. He also longed to find the opportunity to respond to an inner voice that grew louder every year, urging him to develop his love of art. At night, after working a twelve-hour day at the farm, he attended animal husbandry classes at the University of Maryland. On Sundays he studied but also drew and worked on sculpting animal figures in clay. His farm wages barely paid for his education, but he studied animal care with an intensity and passion that made the eating of regular meals and the getting of sleep at night very low on his list of priorities. He was obsessed with getting ahead and with making enough money to give him time to explore the world of art.

By the time Ed was twenty-one years old, he already had raised and shown "the Supreme Grand Champion Guernsey Bull." I once read a diary entry he made at the time, in which he wrote, "I have won my Nobel Prize." At twenty-one he had achieved in the cattle world what it takes most people a lifetime to accomplish, if they ever get there at all.

Knowledge of Ed's tough childhood made Mama's maternal instincts spring forth with vigor. She wanted nothing more than to mother him, and he loved it. She became his surrogate mother. It brought tears to her eyes when Ed sang sentimental songs to her in his deep, resonant baritone. It didn't matter to her that he was tone deaf and completely off key.

Although my mother was on my side during my romance with Ed, my brothers gave him a hard time, as was the custom in Italian families. It was expected. No one was supposed to be "good enough" for one's sister. Two of my brothers came home on leave one weekend just to check out this man who was spending so much time with their sister. I remember the long discussions behind closed doors, during which my brothers asked Ed exactly what his intentions were toward me. By now Ed was prepared. He told them what his aspirations were, how little money he made at present, but that he understood the work ethic and would always take care of me. In the meantime, Mama was busy in the kitchen making Ed's favorite oyster stew, sweet potato pie, and applesauce cake. This was not a traditional family meal but Mama's way of celebrating the engagement of her daughter.

During the weeks following his visits to Brooklyn, we wrote long love letters to each other every day. The mailman regularly greeted me or Mama saying, "Well, well. *He's* written again!" Ed always decorated his envelopes with colorful drawings of prancing Percherons, love birds, and other creatures. Sometimes his romantic notes even had naughty little drawings on the inside that neither the mailman nor Mama ever knew about.

Finally a letter arrived that said simply, "It's time. Let's get married."

I wrote back one word—"Yes." It wasn't very romantic the way he phrased it, but "Let's get married" was all I cared about.

We planned to be married on Sunday, October 29, 1944, but just a few days beforehand, Ed and his fellow soldiers received word that some of them would be shipped overseas the following Monday. The final list of those going would not be posted until early Saturday evening, less than twenty-four hours before the wedding ceremony.

Of course, Mama and I had already made all the arrangements. The invitations had been mailed; the traditional wedding dress, previously worn by my two sisters, was ready; and, of course, Mama had prepared the food. We were beside ourselves with worry, but there was nothing we could do. I felt my entire future was in the hands of God and the United States Air Force.

Ed promised me he would be on the last train from Pawling Saturday night if his name was *not* on the list of those going overseas.

I waited at the gate at Grand Central Station for the 12:04 from upstate New York. It was cold and wet in the station, and it was the longest hour of my entire life. As the passengers got off the train, I saw his familiar figure in the distance, loaded down with several green duffel bags that could very well have contained his clothes for the wedding, his clothes for the honeymoon, and perhaps a small animal or two besides.

We hugged each other, and I called Mama with the good news that the wedding was on. That night we went to our first nightclub to see Billy Rose's "Long-Stem Roses" at the Copacabana, and I had my first champagne. I must have looked like a silly teenager, I was so excited to be there. Ed and I didn't dance. Ballroom dancing was something I was going to have to teach him first, but of course, I never did. The tall chorus girls, the "Long-Stem Roses" as they were called, were beautiful, but we only had eyes for each other.

At 3:30 that morning I went to bed in the room I shared with my mother. I was still a proper member of the family.

The next day, October 29, 1944, we were married at St. Mary's Roman Catholic Church in Bensonhurst, Brooklyn.

Like everything connected with Ed Boehm, our wedding was

not to be a normal, surprise-free, standard occasion. At one point I thought it was not even going to take place. Unknown to me, Ed had indeed arrived at the church on time. But then he kept me waiting for almost half an hour, and naturally I thought that he had changed his mind. The guests evidently were thinking the same thing; there was a terrible restlessness in the church. I kept waiting for the signal that would start me down the aisle. It did not come. I could hear people in the church whispering. Had he gotten cold feet? Was he afraid to face me? I was frantic, frightened, and then just plain mad. Finally Ed appeared.

"Have you been milking a cow? Or is one of your roosters lame this time?" I asked when I met him at the foot of the altar. There was a steel edge to my voice.

"You never told me the pastor knew so much about cattle and horses!" he whispered excitedly. "We've been comparing notes."

The wedding ceremony was beautiful, in spite of its unusual beginning. When making plans for the wedding, Ed had insisted on substituting his favorite popular song, "I Believe," for the traditional "Ave Maria." It was a song associated with overly sentimental teenagers who burst into torrents of tears at the first strains of the melody. Mama and I were mortified. In those days, changing the church music was tantamount to sacrilege, but we gave in after he pleaded, "But Helen, I do believe in what it says!"

One hundred people came to the reception and ate Mama's lasagna and veal *alla Milanese,* along with those lovely pastel-colored sugar almonds tucked into little tulle pouches that are an Italian custom at weddings. The reception had a bittersweet air because many of the men were in uniform and several were leaving immediately to go overseas.

In marrying Ed, I knew that animals were going to be a part of our marriage, but how many brides have their grooms leave them on their honeymoon for an entire night to go coon hunting with old friends? Ed did this to me the second night we were married. At one o'clock in the morning he came back into the bedroom full of joy and excitement. He had caught a live raccoon and brought the smelly animal with him. I took one look at it and dashed into the bathroom.

"I'm not coming out until you get that creature out of *our* bedroom!" I shouted through the door. "This is our honeymoon, Edward Marshall Boehm. I never thought I'd have to compete with a raccoon!"

Something in my voice convinced him to expel the raccoon from our bedroom—but not before first giving it a saucer of milk.

Ed was stunned that anyone would react to a live animal in such a hostile manner. I was to learn before long that his priorities revolved around animals, fish, birds, flowers—anything at all to do with nature.

Little did I know then that an endless sequence of heated and reheated dinners was in store for me. Ed could hold visitors enthralled until two in the morning discussing the relative intelligence of a hummingbird compared to that of a warbler. A guest would have to display passionate interest in topics such as hummingbirds, pheasants, or sheepdogs to capture Ed's attention. I gradually came to understand his nature lover's fear that it was all going to disappear some day. The thirty-eight dogs, hundreds of fish and plant species, and thousands of birds we later had in our possession never quelled his appetite for the flora and fauna he loved so much. If I was to love Ed, I would also have to love all the flora and fauna. The raccoon taught me that.

5

Starting Out Together

The war ended a few months after our wedding, and we moved into Mama's large house. Mama loved having Ed added to our household. Our family had had a small dog or maybe a cat now and then when we were growing up, but pets had never altered the household routine. Within a few days' time, Mama allowed Ed to move a fish tank into the middle of the living room. Next came a huge Alsatian dog that repelled Mama at first. "It's to protect Helen in case she wants to go out at night for a little fresh air," he lied. Mama gradually grew to accept and even to love the Alsatian.

One day, the fish tank sprang a leak and drained over the entire living room rug. We came home after work to the smell of wet carpeting and to the sight of dead fish on the waterless floor of the tank. Ed was devastated at losing his fish; Mama was devastated by the ruination of her carpet and wood floor.

But even that disaster didn't keep Mama from allowing Ed anything he wanted. If it was outrageous, which it almost always was, he would prove so persuasive that she would relent from any opposition. When my brothers had special requests, they had no easy time getting Mama to grant them. But Ed Boehm! For example, Mama's southern Italian cooking included oil, not butter, and certainly nothing as exotic as oysters. But if Ed wanted oyster stew with butter, that's what we ate. ("Oysters!" exclaimed my startled brothers. "How did *they* get in this house?")

At first, I continued as Dr. Gillis's receptionist in Brooklyn. Not only did I love watching Dr. Gillis grind glasses and expertly fit his clients, but I was fascinated with the entire ordering process, which taught me all about the various optical houses and fashionable frame makers.

Sometimes when business was slow and the doctor was out of the office, I'd dash into the back room and experiment on old lenses that had been tossed aside.

One afternoon, Dr. Gillis returned early from lunch and found me bent over the long laboratory table, concentrating on making holes in an old pair of lenses with a diamond drill. I looked up, startled and embarrassed. He was delighted.

"Well, Helen, it appears as though you have a real knack for this—more than for being just receptionist. I've been aware of your feelings of ambition for some time now. Why don't you take some courses at my son's school in Brooklyn Heights? Then you could assist me in filling prescriptions."

The idea appealed to me. Becoming an optician would mean both career advancement and more money. It was a field in which women could achieve. I had learned a good business lesson at an early age: Go where the money is. There would always be a market for helping people with their eyes, so in the evenings I took classes at the Mechanical School of Optics in Brooklyn Heights, where I studied optics and eye fashion.

I guess the old adage about working hard and succeeding is often true. Within the year I had become one of the first women in New York licensed as a dispensing optician. I looked on my job as the second of my career triumphs (before I had secretly considered myself a dress designer). I felt the same sense of elation at receiving my optician's license, number 495, as when I'd won first prize for the design of my junior high school graduation dress. Those were two occasions in my early life when the sweet taste of self-recognition was mine to enjoy.

In the meantime, Ed's life also had taken an unexpected change. All during the war years he had looked forward to returning to managing the large Guernsey breeding farm in Maryland that he had left to enter the air force, but a terrible fire had completely destroyed the farm while he was in the service, leaving him without a position to which to return. He'd spent fifteen years of his life living, breathing, and studying animals. All of his research, his breeding records—everything—had vanished in the fire. It meant finding another job, and he finally found one as assistant to a well-known veterinarian in Great Neck, Long Island. We took the tiny apartment over the vet's office and left Mama's house.

Ed enjoyed taking care of sick animals. He had a special affinity for them, and I was convinced that his skill in diagnosing the ailments of his animal patients and in determining their cures often exceeded that of his employer. Ed seemed to me in a way like Saint Francis of Assisi. Animals would come to him; even birds would come to him. He knew how to imitate their sounds and how to communicate with them. I had never seen another human being with such a natural and instinctive feeling for the animal world.

Those first months in Great Neck were not what I had expected married life to be. Our apartment was always jammed with Ed's clay sculptures, our possessions, and live creatures. We had very little money, and I had a tough daily commute to my job.

Life with Ed was never without surprise. He had a wonderful sense of humor and was always unpredictable. I never knew what he would say or do next. He left me not just constantly surprised but almost always delighted. Throughout our courtship, he had said, "Helen, I promise you, I'll always be a headache, but I'll never be a bore." And he lived up to that one hundred percent.

Not long after he took the job with the vet, I realized he was unhappy routinely working for someone from 8 A.M. until 5 P.M., even though he was very fond of the doctor. Ed was the independent type. He believed in working when there was work to be done, even if it meant in the small hours of the morning. He was willing to stay up all night with a sick animal, consoling it and treating it. But he wanted to be his own man, work his own hours, so I knew our life could not stay the way it was.

I don't think many brides had my problems in those days. Our apartment was a mini-zoo. Ed brought home one stray animal after another. His idea of marvelous self-indulgence was to spend his entire paycheck on a pair of beautiful fowl or kissing gouramis (tropical fish). Needless to say, I didn't view those additions in quite the same way Ed did. We were on such a tight budget that I used to stay up nights candling eggs in exchange for groceries. When I saw those kissing gouramis swimming in their tank, I visualized all the sacks of groceries for which they were a substitute, including lovely marbled steaks whose juicy flavor I could taste just by thinking about it! Meanwhile Ed was like a little boy, exclaiming over the beauty and rarity of the creatures he'd found and purchased. We could wait for the marbled steaks.

We would have made a wonderful television sitcom series, because husband and wife spent night after night grooming dogs, combing fowl, feeding animals in the yellow and black kitchen, and/or stepping over any number of crawling creatures. We'd have dinner in our kitchen, and only while drinking coffee at the end of the meal would Ed announce sheepishly that he'd brought home another very special pet and left it in the back yard. I'd rush down into the back yard for a look, and it would always be something unexpected, like a huge Doberman pinscher. Then he'd bring the dog inside, pose her, and make *me* hold her steady on the kitchen table while he sculpted her in clay. I learned not to be scared; I had never had much experience with animals, but I realized it was either love and live with the animals and be their friend or leave Ed Boehm. I loved him so much that I felt I could learn to love the other part of his life, even if it included a menagerie of creatures that walked, jumped, or flew. Ed's superb control over animals taught me assurance in handling them myself, and I completely overcame my fear of large animals during the first year of our marriage.

Ed continued to sculpt and make clay models of dogs, horses, fowl, birds, cattle, and other examples of wild life. Soon our entire apartment was filled with these sculptures, and there was hardly any room for our own things any more. I watched Ed come home at night exhausted from his veterinarian duties and then turn to his hardest work—his art—with a passion so intense that I knew this must be his future life's work. We sat down at our little table and talked long into the night about his need to change his career path. I encouraged him to visit museums and to learn more about the craft, and he talked of his dream of eventually opening his own studio.

Months later, after intensive research into the various types of sculpture, Ed told me he had come to a decision. His material was to be hard-paste porcelain. His selection of the porcelain medium was based on his love of color as well as form in the natural world. Bronze, stone, metal, and wood did not meet his criteria. Ed wanted to express the piercing look of an eagle, the soulful glance in the eye of a cow or a cocker, the softness of a feather. Porcelain, with its full spectrum of colors and glazes, was the only possible choice.

Porcelain had never been a recognized American art form, although for centuries the Chinese and Europeans had excelled in it. In order to work in hard-paste (high-fired) porcelain, he would need a large studio, and that would require large sums of money. Since we were just making ends meet on his and my salary, this seemed just a fantasy. In the meanwhile, something happened in my own career that was going to help Ed in a way neither of us could have predicted.

6

"If Meyrowitz Is the Finest, Then Why Aren't You Working There?"

"Who is the finest optician in New York?" my husband asked me one night. He was tending a sick Leghorn rooster in our kitchen, preparing it for the National Fancy Fowl Show in the Armory in New York City.

"Meyrowitz on Fifth Avenue," I replied. "I always go there to buy instruments and equipment for Dr. Gillis. In fact, I have to go there tomorrow on a mission for Dr. Gillis."

Meyrowitz was undoubtedly the leading international optical center, and some of the world's great opthalmologists went there regularly to purchase their instruments. It was a beautiful place. On the first floor there were rows of shiny mahogany desks with maroon leather tops and very handsome mirrors. The opticians all looked very aristocratic, and their clients were the most elegant people in New York.

Measuring some medicine for his rooster with an eye dropper; Ed asked me quietly, "If Meyrowitz is the finest, then why aren't you working there?"

"Oh, Ed. They'd never employ a woman."

He looked at me. "Helen, you are going to be the best in the business. I want you working with the nicest kind of people, serving the best clientele. You could grow and learn more about your field there than anywhere else."

The next morning I put on my best white uniform and took the train to New York, full of enthusiasm and determined to try to get a job at Meyrowitz. It was just after the war, and opticians were in short supply.

I pulled open the large glass door and stepped inside. There were low-hanging chandeliers, and the voices of the people inside were muted because of the thick wool carpet. A haughty voice greeted me. It was the receptionist.

"May I help you?"

"I'd like to see Mr. Cook, the president."

"Whatever for?" Her eyes gave me a very cool appraisal.

"About employment."

"We don't need any secretaries."

"I'm not a secretary. I'm here to see about a position as a dispensing optician. I am qualified and I am certain Mr. Cook could use me."

The receptionist reluctantly sent me in to the president's office, and there, sitting at a great rolltop desk, was an awesome, very stern-looking man dressed in an impeccable pinstriped suit with a gold watch chain draped across his ample waist. He had a large white handlebar moustache, which he twisted as he listened to me ask for employment. (He reminded me of my paternal grandfather, from pictures I had seen.) He also looked very skeptical.

"A woman? Well, how exactly do you think we can use you?" His tone sounded more like, "How presumptuous—asking the great guild opticians for employment."

I realized I had to sell myself right out of DeKalb Avenue and Bedford onto glamorous Fifth Avenue. It was the beginning of a lifetime career of selling. I had to persuade Mr. Cook that I would be a great addition to his staff, that I could fit glasses and fill prescriptions, that I had a working knowledge of every aspect of optical laboratory work. I also had a great deal of experience assisting Dr. Gillis in the ordering of his equipment—and from Meyrowitz itself, which was famous everywhere for its extraordinary inventory of optical and surgical supplies.

"Mr. Cook, I know you'd be pleased with my work. I'm very conscientious, and I've had several years of experience." We talked some more.

He twirled his moustache some more, plucked his watch from his vest and studied it, then looked at me and thought for what seemed like an eternity. Finally, he stood up and shook my hand. I had the job.

And thus I became one of New York's first registered female opticians with the prestigious firm of Meyrowitz, with branches in London and Paris. From DeKalb Avenue and Bedford to Fifth Avenue! I had done what Ed had challenged me to do: I had found a job with "the best." Working there would give me the opportunity to meet influential people, and one of those people would change our lives forever. In the meantime, I was dreaming of London and Paris.

Downstairs with the Boys,
Upstairs with the King

I was Meyrowitz's first woman employee in the laboratory. It was my first really important job, but it was not yet to be my moment of glory. I was not given the honor of being seated at one of the desks beneath the chandeliers on the thick-carpeted first floor.

Instead, I was given a desk in the basement. As Mr. Cook explained, "We just can't put a woman optician on the main floor, handling our clients' prescriptions just like that."

My first important but rather tedious assignment was as "inspector of prescriptions," which meant that I had to make certain every prescription was properly filled. My colleagues were thirty-nine men, clad in T-shirts and blue aprons, grinding lenses to the constant splash of water. Occasionally they would forget I was around and slip into a torrent of rich obscenities.

I was resented at first. I had crashed their male domain. They didn't like having to watch their language around me, but after the first two months we became friends, and after the first year, they were friendly, caring coworkers. They worked hard, standing in pools of water and flint and grinding their lenses while I sat at my table and checked and then rechecked several hundred lenses a day through my lensometer. Then, via a dumbwaiter, I

34

would dispatch the glasses, with prescriptions attached, to the "other world" of the main floor.

We never saw the people who purchased the glasses that were our daily responsibility, but we heard their famous names via the grapevine—Ginger Rogers, Kay Francis, Broadway stars, shahs, sheiks, and princesses. We moved with great speed down in the basement, working to please the male opticians who sat one floor up clad in their three-piece suits and leaning on the beautiful leather-topped tables. I knew I was learning a great many things, but it was still a frustration not to know what was going on right above our heads in that other world.

Finally my break came, a year and a half after I had started my job. Several of the opticians had not come into work one day because there was a flu epidemic. It was always very busy during the noon hour, and Mr. Cook became frantic. Something had to be done about all the clients who were waiting. *No one* was supposed to be kept waiting at Meyrowitz's!

I always wore a dress beneath my blue working smock. Mr. Cook told me to remove my smock and come upstairs to help out with the clients. This was the chance I had been waiting for—to wait on real people, most of them prominent personalities. This was the taste of dignity and professional pride for which I had been waiting.

I sat down behind the elegant desk-table, calmed my trembling hands, and proceeded to greet my customers with as much aplomb as I could muster. The noon rush hour whizzed by very quickly, and then I was banished downstairs again. It was not to be for long. I became a regular upstairs substitute until the day an Indian businessman and his sari-clad wife sat opposite me to order "a few little items" they needed. Their "needs," including a number of solid gold frames and a pair of gilt binoculars, added up to a sale of $2,700, one of Meyrowitz's largest in several years. Even Mr. Cook was stunned. It was soon after that he told me I could "stay upstairs." It was a victory for me, but I felt it was also a victory for women in my field.

The customers liked me. I guess it was partly the big grin on my face that made them "feel better," as one elderly gentleman described it. I used a combination of imagination and fashion sense to make the selection of a frame a serious exercise, whether I was working on the frame of an Arab sheik or a debutante, a dowager grandmother or a Wall Street scion. In those days, that approach was altogether new. I made the customer's decision "as exciting as buying a car," one man laughingly told me.

I even knew how to start fads in frames. I liked one new model—tortoiseshell with fourteen-karat gold hinges—so much that, because of my enthusiasm in recommending it, people all over the city began to wear them and to cause others to want them. Customers began calling me "Helen" and asked for me when they came in. Since I was conspicuous as the only woman, it was a kind of reverse discrimination.

I was destined to outsell the men. I was born enthusiastic, and when a customer sat across from me, there always seemed to be an extra supply of energy upon which to draw. This was a talent I would later put to excellent use in selling my husband's porcelains. When the Meyrowitz client was an attractive woman, I would suggest that she purchase two pairs of glasses, not just one, for she would need a "dazzling" pair for evening and something more studious or businesslike for her daytime image. Often as not, I would sell her four pairs of glasses—two for daytime, two for evening—so that in case of loss she would always have a proper pair available to use. (I was already, it seems, an advocate of conspicuous consumption!)

On an otherwise normal day, the men and I were busily writing up orders during a brief lull. Suddenly I noticed a strange silence. I looked up in time to see them all beating a soft-footed retreat to the back room. My heart sank. The men always left the really famous people to me—one of their boyish pranks. As I turned toward the entrance wondering who it might be this time, a familiar figure walked purposefully toward me.

It was Bernard Baruch, the famous financial adviser to presidents and, incidentally, lover to several very famous women. I opened my mouth to greet him, but no words emerged. I coughed and somehow found my voice, managing a quavery "Oh, Mr. Baruch, please sit down." The little pince-nez wobbling on his nose needed adjusting.

At first I was afraid to touch them. If I broke them, it would take two weeks to replace them because the prescription was so unusual.

Finally, I stood up and, with my heart in my mouth, removed the glasses, carefully made two adjustments with my little pliers, and set them back on his famous nose.

"How are they now, Mr. Baruch?"

"*Fine,* young lady, fine! You did a good job!" And with that he tucked his *Wall Street Journal* smartly under his arm and walked out.

Although I pretended to swear vengeance on the other salesmen, the incident strengthened my tie to them and earned me even greater respect. I knew Mr. Cook was pleased, because after that Mrs. Cook herself would ask me to wait on her and her friends.

I celebrated my fifth anniversary at Meyrowitz the very day the world's most handsome man, Clark Gable, strolled through the revolving glass doors. There was no doubt about it—this customer was to be mine. I shot up from my chair, moved quickly to the figure in the beige cashmere overcoat, and said, "Mr. Gable, please step this way." The male opticians did not stand a chance; I had him by the arm before any of the others had even risen from their seats. After all, I stepped aside when glamorous female movie stars came through the Meyrowitz doors, so the men could not complain.

Mr. Cook, in his careful instructions on how to measure clients for glasses, stressed one cardinal rule that we were never to break: We were not, under any circumstances, to touch the client more than was absolutely necessary.

The day Clark Gable appeared there were no rules, as far as I was concerned. I spent twice as much time as was necessary moving my hands about that handsome face. He was incredible-looking, with a faint smile that never left his lips and crinkled up the corners of his eyes. He seemed permanently amused. His ears were slightly too big, but what woman would care about a minor detail like that?

He wanted a "simple pair of sunglasses." I was not going to make this a simple occasion, I decided, watching him remove his coat and silk scarf. He sat down and said, "Well?"

He was waiting for me to say something. I saw a flash of pure white teeth in a lovely smile.

"Do you have a prescription, Mr. Gable?"

"Well, young lady, before we discuss that, tell me, what's your name?" His sonorous baritone startled me. It sounded as it should have sounded, just like in the movies.

"Helen Boehm, sir." My voice trailed off. I was hoping he wouldn't notice my frantic signs to my colleagues to take our picture with the new Polaroid camera we'd just got in the store.

"Mrs. Boehm, I don't need a prescription. I just want a pair of sunglasses."

"May I suggest, Mr. Gable," I said, summoning up my most professional tone, "collapsible tortoiseshell glasses, just like the ones the racing car drivers wear? They've just arrived from Paris, and their size after collapsing will not overstuff your pocket."

"Well, that sounds very interesting," he said. "Maybe I should change my profession." Then he laughed. "Will these make me drive my own car any better or faster?"

I could feel the heat on my blushing cheeks. "No. I mean . . . er . . . a lot of men simply like the image of a race car driver."

He put his head back and let out a bellowing laugh. Everyone in the shop was mesmerized. "All right, Mrs. Boehm, let's make me a racing car driver," he boomed.

"Oh, Mr. Gable," I implored, "these ready-made frames we have just aren't good enough for you. *You* need something special." And I began to measure his pupilary distance. At 75½, it was the largest I'd ever seen. This was something to tell Mr. Cook and the men about, though I soon discovered it mattered a lot less to them than it did to me. Then I measured his bridge, his temple, all around the ears, and every other place I could think of. Not a single measurement, of course, was needed for his sunglasses; this was purely my little scheme to delay his visit.

"If I'm fired for this," I thought as I looked into those marvelous hazel eyes, which crinkled up completely because of a very broad smile, "it will be worth it!"

While this totally unnecessary charade of mine was going on, complete with a fine string and a millimeter ruler, the other women in the store—all the telephone operators, secretaries, receptionists—were strung along the balcony that overlooked the main floor, staring down immobilized at the scene.

When I had finished measuring "the King," as he was known then, he stood up, adjusted his silk tie in a wall mirror, and took my hand to say good-bye.

"Oh, Mr. Gable, I almost forgot. We have a selection of colors for the frames. Would you prefer demi-blond or demi-amber in the tortoiseshell?"

He paused for a moment. I half expected him to say, "Frankly, my dear, I don't give a damn." But he was much more polite to me than to Scarlett O'Hara. "Well, Mrs. Boehm, I'll leave the selection of the color entirely up to you."

He smiled broadly again. "I never in my life thought it would take so long to get a pair of sunglasses!"

"Quality, Mr. Gable, takes longer."

"And creating an image?" He winked and let my hand go.

I watched the handsome figure receding through the door, on his way to meet his present wife, Lady Ashley. Every pair of eyes followed him. For months afterward I described this encounter to anyone who would listen. Women kept asking me to repeat the story; they regarded me with envy. I claimed to Ed that I had achieved a certain fame in our neighborhood in Great Neck. Ed, of course, simply didn't understand what the fuss was all about. Now, if it had been an exquisite specimen of a mynah bird, well, that would have been something to talk about. But Clark Gable?

We Find a Benefactor

The next five years were a very happy time in my life. My marriage to Ed obviously was the most important thing that would ever happen to me. He made me content. He told me that I was beautiful and wonderful. No one but Mama had ever told me that before. He gave me self-confidence, and I gave confidence back to him. Whenever he felt depressed about how slowly things were going, I smiled my brightest, made him laugh, and made him feel we could conquer the world together. Half the time I was kidding myself, too, but in expressing hope and optimism I almost made myself believe it. We needed each other, we delighted in each other's company, and somehow nothing would defeat us.

Our strength together was amazing, considering how independent we both were. I spent my days working on clients' eyesight problems and my evenings with Ed, helping him with the medical problems of his menagerie of animals, which he led me to believe were far more important than my human clients. We were not the normal, everyday young American couple!

Money was tight. We planned, dreamed, and saved, never knowing what direction our lives would take in the future. I wanted Ed to become an artist, because I saw the excitement in his eyes when he found the time to use his fingers and modeling tools in creating the most lifelike of animals. He kept trying to push the idea of being a full-time artist out of his consciousness, because he said it would be "complete, total economic suicide." I was the devil's advocate. I kept bringing his dream to the fore, reminding him over and over again that "when we do it, this will be your future."

Although we were traveling down two separate highways at the time—Ed with his animals and I with my optician's career—we knew that the energy we could create as a team working toward the same goal was just plain explosive. Somehow there *had* to be a way in which my husband could devote himself to the life of an artist and I could help him as his partner. We would have to find a way.

Ed finally had the courage to make the big decision. He resigned his job as assistant to the vet. We now had one small salary to live on—mine. The rest of Ed's life was to be dedicated to his art, but this step was not a rejection of his beloved animals. They would continue to be a part of both our lives.

We were babes in the woods in the world of porcelain art, but I was sure we would make it. The first portent of success came almost immediately; Herbert Hazeltine, the world-renowned sculptor, took Ed as his student and protegé. The chance to work under Hazeltine was an honor many artists would have fought for. Ed assisted him with his great classic cast of Man O' War, perhaps the most famous race horse in world history. Ed watched and learned and admired as Hazeltine went through all the meticulous, difficult steps in developing this masterpiece from a first rough sketch to the final bronze, a magnificent sculpture of a magnificent animal, bathed in a golden patina. Ed talked in his sleep for three nights about Man O' War, and it haunted him through his life.

This was a period in which Ed routinely came home elated, stimulated, and exhausted. Along with studying with the great master, he did research in the stacks of public and museum libraries on the art of porcelain-making in ancient civilizations. I saw precious little of him during these months, and I shed some private tears more than once, wondering whether he had made the right decision to leave his job. But the decision had been made. *Les jeux sont faits, mesdames et messieurs.*

Ed not only worked all day and night during the week, but on weekends he took the train to Trenton, a ceramics center, leaving early Saturday morning and returning to Great Neck Sunday night. Saturday nights he stayed with the Hollendonner family, friends in Trenton who had a mold shop and helped him with his mold of a cocker spaniel sculpture. When he was ready to fire it, he used the test kilns at United Clay Mines, researching the ancient way of handling clay. He tested and tried again and again, toiling away like some mythical magician. When, many years later, I visited the Chinese birthplace of porcelain, I could not help remembering those days early in our marriage when Ed struggled to recreate the ancient, ingenious Chinese formula at the United Clay Mines in New Jersey.

The night that he told me he had finally unlocked the secret of making hard-paste porcelain was an historic moment for us. He came home on a Sunday night and told me he had a surprise that he would not reveal until dinner. I hurriedly prepared our meal, and we sat down at our little kitchen table with a candle burning in the empty Chianti bottle.

"Ed, come on, what's the surprise?" I was dying of curiosity. Since Ed never gave me presents, I thought that maybe this was one time he had found a trinket for me in a pawnshop.

"Helen," he said, his eyes creased with exhaustion lines but bright with excitement, too, "I've found it. I know now how to make the kind of porcelain I need to make my sculptures!"

The British finding Tutankhamen's tomb felt no greater excitement than the Boehms did that night in Great Neck, Long Island. I hugged him, and we laughed and toasted each other with red wine. It was a celebration we would never forget. We stayed at that kitchen table after the dishes were done and plotted and planned our business and our future until the sun rose.

There was to be no more crystal-ball gazing. There wasn't time for that. We knew exactly where we were going. We were going to gamble that we could penetrate a market—the American market—that hitherto had bought only English, European, and Asian porcelains. Neither of us realized what an overwhelming goal we were setting for ourselves. We only felt that we could do anything we set our minds and hearts to do. We accepted the

English, European, and Asian ceramist challenge. If they had dominated the field exclusively for thousands of years, well then it was our turn.

Talk about chutzpah. We had it—and then some! The boy who'd grown up in a Maryland orphanage and the girl who'd grown up in an Italian immigrant's Brooklyn house were taking on several continents. If youthful enthusiasm, determination, and the ability to work ten-hour days seven days a week would help assure success, then we would succeed. We were a team: two opposites—a shy artist and his aggressive salesperson wife— but together we made a whole. We were a dynamic force that simply would not be checked.

We now had the knowledge, the product, and the enthusiasm. There was something lacking, however, in our enterprise: money. Together Ed and I timidly approached a veterinarian for whom Ed had worked. By lending us $500, he put us in business. We naturally included the cocker in the first group of porcelains—all of dogs—which we christened "Champions on Parade." While Ed made the dogs, I fed the artist and sold the dogs, too. Our small apartment had by now become a business office, sculptor's studio, home for stray animals, and a place where excellent pasta was cooked.

It was painful watching Ed spend such incredibly long hours creating his exquisite, one-of-a-kind sculptures for only a handful of buyers. Our backer, like many, expected immediate results for his money, which was impossible. Within a surprisingly short time our first venture, "Champions on Parade," was dissolved. Our "champions" had become losers. Ed, who possessed little business acumen, was deeply discouraged. I decided I had to be confident for both of us, and tenacious as well. I knew another break would come along, but I couldn't just sit back and let a miracle happen. I had to make it happen and make it happen now.

By now I had met numerous celebrities and rich people in my work at Meyrowitz. I became determined to find the money to allow Ed to continue his work. I researched my clients, found one who was particularly well-heeled, and then decided to summon my courage to attack. Before doing that, however, I felt I had to discuss it with Ed. He looked at me with disbelief. It was so completely impossible to do from his point of view that he shook his head and said, "Helen, it won't work." He should have known me better by then.

My target was a man from the Midwest who came in several times a year to buy four or five pairs of our most costly glasses. I used to wonder what he did with all the pairs he must have broken, but I always enjoyed seeing him and was glad he kept on breaking or losing them. He was the head of a large conglomerate and sat on several important corporate boards.

I had spent a lot of time talking business with him during the years he had been my client. He wore expensive clothes, a Philippe Patek watch, and a small gold seal ring and had manicured fingernails. He obviously was a man of means. More importantly, he was a man of compassion. He always inquired about Ed on his visits and asked how the sculpture work was progressing. I knew he was involved in twelve corporations already—why not thirteen?

When his appointment day arrived, I felt suddenly intimidated. My client could become angry; my boss, Mr. Cook, could fire me. There were a lot of possible negatives. The most intimidating of all, of course, was the good chance that the client would say no to me.

Our future benefactor, wearing his familiar cashmere coat (like the one Clark Gable wore, I kept remembering), strode through the Fifth Avenue door and headed directly toward my desk. We exchanged greetings and a few words of small talk. Then, as I adjusted the new glasses, I got to the point.

"If you don't mind," I began, "I would like to talk with you about a personal matter. My husband has just developed a method for making fine porcelain that's very close to the methods used by the ancient Chinese. We're very excited about the success."

"Congratulations, Mrs. Boehm."

"We're hoping to open a small studio." I paused only long enough to catch a breath. "You're an astute businessman, and I thought you might want the opportunity to be part of the only hard-paste porcelain studio in this country."

Another pause while I watched his face closely for any sign of interest. His gray eyes were cool; he gave no sign of reaction.

"It would make an excellent investment," I assured him. "You'll make money."

"Young lady," he finally said, half-amused, half-irritated. "What on earth are you talking about? A porcelain studio? I'm in the flour business. I own national bakeries, and the only thing I know about figurines is that the bric-a-brac my wife puts all over the place is difficult to dust."

That really turned on the spigot. Out came a rush of explanations. I would not let him interrupt. I told him how important this was going to be, how we knew our market, how well I could sell, how we were going to make this the biggest success in the world of fine art since Marco Polo had opened the trade route to the Far East.

He finally interrupted my sales pitch, the speed of which had risen to a race level. "Mrs. Boehm, Mrs. Boehm," he said, his face now wreathed in a big smile. "Look, I'm late. You don't have to sell me anymore. Look, put some data on paper, send it to me at my office, and I'll have my accountants look it over. Maybe I could participate . . . in a small way. If they agree, I'll send you a check. At any rate, congratulate your husband and tell him I'm interested."

I wanted to lean over the tabletop and kiss him then and there, I was so overcome with relief and joy. But the solemn figure of Mr. Cook lurking in the background brought me to my senses.

That night, after my chicken *alla Romana* dinner, as always cooked according to Mama's exact instructions, Ed and I worked into the morning hours, formulating our modest proposal. Ten thousand dollars was our suggestion as a requirement to start up the venture. We mailed the proposal together with an agreement drawn up by our neighbor, an attorney, one of those wonderful friends in life who know not to send the bill for their work "right now."

Time passed. I called Ed from Meyrowitz each day when I knew the mail had arrived. Each day another disappointment. No news. We gave up hope of my customer's assistance. Then, about five weeks later, to our amazement, both a check and the signed agreement arrived in the mail.

There it was. One thousand dollars! We didn't know then if

the additional $9,000 was forthcoming, but $1,000 already seemed like a fortune to us, the beginning of a new life. We called our new company the Osso China Company (*osso* means "bone" in Italian). (We kept this name until early in 1951, when we reacted to the buyers' desire to know who designed the porcelain animals they purchased. At that point we changed the company name to Edward Marshall Boehm, Inc.)

The thousand dollars went for a basement studio on Stokes Avenue in Trenton. There we were, in the heart of the porcelain industry in America. We were in business finally in the fall of 1949.

In the following months, additional monies came from our benefactor, but only for the necessary purchases of equipment and materials I pleaded for in my constant letters. He probably never had a major investment deal that took as much of his time as our transactions, but I think we were his comic relief for the day. In any case, I shall never forget him, because he gave us our chance.

It was now time to move to Trenton. The commute for Ed from Great Neck was too taxing, particularly since he often worked until well past midnight. In the spring of 1950, we packed our meager belongings and Ed's precious sculptures and closed the door for the last time on our first apartment.

The night before we left Great Neck for our new apartment in Lawrenceville, New Jersey, we decided to have two of our neighbors over for dinner. We'd never been able to entertain anyone, as we hadn't time or money for that purpose, but we somehow felt we shouldn't leave without extending a friendly gesture. After all, we wanted to appear like your normal couple, even if we knew we weren't.

When they arrived, I was struck by the wife's extremely good-looking coat, which had a lovely full fox collar, and I laid it out very carefully on the bed in our room. We ate dinner in a little corner I'd managed to carve out of our tiny living room, on a card table covered with a cloth, candles, wineglasses, and Mama's silver. It was a wonderfully cozy evening, and I wondered why I hadn't tried to do this more often.

When it was time for them to go, I went into the bedroom to get the coat. There was the collar, partially stripped from the coat and somewhat mutilated. Purring contentedly atop a pile of fox fur was our Persian cat.

I was horrified. I walked out in a daze with the coat in my arms, ready to explain the incident. The wife, however, took one look at the bedraggled object and instantly proceeded to blame her huge boxer at home for the damage. "It must have happened when I laid it on the sofa and went back upstairs for my keys," she moaned, putting us off the hook.

The neighbors in our area must have been relieved to see us go. One of them told me that she was going to miss "the Boehm zoo with all its crowing roosters, screeching birds, and barking dogs," because she had grown used to it. (Her comment caused Ed to remark that she was obviously a person of discernment.)

I now was the one with the tough commute. In order to get to Meyrowitz's, I drove from Lawrenceville to Trenton to catch the train. At Penn Station I boarded the IRT subway for Fifth Avenue and then walked to the store. On the morning trip I would do paperwork for our company, but in the evening I would nap in order to arrive home refreshed, ready to cook dinner and greet Ed. Cooking was not one of Ed's interests, even though he occasionally tried. In the second year of our marriage, he'd proudly cooked a duck according to a gourmet recipe he had cut out of the *New York Times*. The only problem was he left the pellets in the duck, and our dinner hour turned into a spitting scene.

I often grabbed a pie for dessert in the indoor shopping mall at Penn Station. I learned to use the station for many of our errands, including dry cleaning and shoe repairs. One night I was loaded with groceries on the train when a heavy snowstorm stopped us in the middle of nowhere. We sat in those cars for eight hours before we were freed. I shared my donuts, cookies, fruit, cheese, and Italian bread with the other hungry passengers in our car. We ate and sang, and in the car ahead of us, a doctor, who was on his way home to New Jersey, delivered a baby.

When I got home to Ed in the wee hours of the morning, he listened to my story and said something that has proven to be quite true: "Helen, wherever you're going to be, there's going to be excitement. Maybe chaos, too, but always excitement. It doesn't happen to you. You create it."

"Ed," I protested, "I did not cause the snowstorm or the birth of the baby."

"No," he smiled, "but you'll always be there when it happens. You have a charmed life."

I guess I have had a charmed life, but I wish Ed could have had one, too. He did not. He was to die at the age of fifty-five, and I was going to have to summon the strength to carry on without him. But at that moment, we did not know what fate had in store for us. We were young, struggling, and full of hope; we "knew" that Ed's gift of God in his hands was going to result in a successful business.

9

Longer Lunch Hours

Come rain or shine, daytime or nighttime, Ed could be found working in his new basement studio. He'd often stay round the clock, taking only a short nap on his cot, in order to finish a porcelain to perfection or to sit with the firing kiln. Whenever I spoke to him about his long absences down in his studio, he'd look at me with such a sense of hurt that I would immediately say, "No, it's all right. It's all right." He had a burning passion that was directed toward just one thing: total mastery of the medium of porcelain in order to create beautiful things that he alone could create.

Only a small number of people knew about his beautiful porcelains, and sales were almost nonexistent. What Ed needed at once was a salesperson. Temperamentally he was not at ease promoting his own work, but he certainly knew the right person for the job—his wife.

I added the role of porcelain salesperson to my life, at first on a small scale.

I started taking a few of Ed's animal porcelains to stores near Meyrowitz to try to sell them on my lunch hour. One day I'd carry the "Hereford Bull" and the "Percheron Stallion" to Black Starr and Gorham, and then to Abercrombie and Fitch or else to Sporting Galleries, and then to Crossroads of Sports—all within

49

walking distance of Meyrowitz. These were heavy, bulky boxes, however, and it was discouraging work. The buyers liked the porcelains, but they demurred at taking any for resale. "Boehm? We've never heard of him." They only wanted English, European, or Asian porcelain. "If it doesn't come from abroad," they'd say, "our customers just won't buy it." The same attitude prevailed among the serious collectors.

One of the buyers for a large department store told me in no uncertain terms, "Young lady, it will take you a hundred years to buck the prestigious names of Minton, Worcester, Wedgwood, Spode, Meissen."

Ed and I didn't have a hundred years.

At this time, he was receiving only about $30 a week from his backer, which meant I certainly had to keep working at Meyrowitz. I was free to present Ed's work to buyers only on my lunch hours, my days off, and periodic weekends. Occasionally I'd dash back to Meyrowitz five or ten minutes late from a lunch hour selling spree. Mr. Cook would check the gold watch at the end of his big chain and then give me one of his famous "looks." He knew exactly what I had been doing.

"Helen, you've got to concentrate on your work here. That's what we pay you for. Or else quit your job and take up running around with that crockery, or whatever it is, full-time."

I apologized and placated him. I would never stop selling Ed's pieces, but I needed my job, too. And then during one lunch hour, the impossible happened: I sold a pair of porcelain wood ducks for $28 to Abercrombie and Fitch and got an order for twenty-five figurines from W. & J. Sloane. Beside myself with excitement, I called Ed long distance to deliver the first encouraging news we'd had since going into business. I also arrived ten minutes late at Meyrowitz, but when I told Mr. Cook about the double sale, he didn't scold me. On the contrary, he looked very, very pleased.

"I feel like I could sell the president of the United States today," I said to Mr. Cook as I quickly sat down at my table.

"Just sell glasses to my customers," he said. "Forget about the president."

When I wasn't selling Ed's work on my lunch hour, I used the time for self-improvement. On some days I would go to the library and read art books. I felt I should be familiar with art terminology, so that I could sound knowledgeable when talking to museums and buyers about Ed's sculptures and art in general. Then I saw a sign in Abercrombie and Fitch's Madison Avenue store announcing that famed golfer Bobby Jones would be giving group golf lessons at lunchtime. I took several of these lessons, even though I had never been on a golf course and perhaps never would be. But I wanted to be prepared, to be able to "talk golf" with the clients Ed and I hoped to land, the owners of the top stores in the country. I wanted to be able to say, "Of course, Bobby Jones told me that I should . . . "

Taking golf lessons from Bobby Jones was very good for my figure, too. It meant I had neither the time nor the money to eat lunch.

One night at supper I happened to mention to Ed that a well-known ophthalmologist, a famous pioneer of the cornea transplant operation, was coming in the next day to purchase operating spectacles. This was an honor for me, since he was so distinguished.

Ed put down his coffee mug on the table with a bang.

"Helen!" he said, his eyes bright with excitement, "you can ask him if he'll remove Otto's cataract!" (Otto was a prized Leghorn rooster.)

I also put down my coffee mug at this remark. "Ed," I said with an undeniable firmness in my voice, "that's an outrageous request, and I would never make it for any reason in this world."

The next day I fitted the doctor's glasses. Then, as he was preparing to stand up to say good-bye, I grabbed his hand with emotion. "You're never going to believe this request, Doctor."

I made the request, he maintained his composure, and three weeks later Ed brought Otto, his prize-winning Leghorn rooster, into the doctor's clinic. Ed sat down with Otto in the waiting room to await their turn with the doctor, as though it were the most normal thing in the world. The other patients in the waiting room that day may have felt more of a need for a psychiatrist than an eye surgeon. But as Ed had predicted, the good doctor took care of Otto with his usual brilliance, and we nursed our patient tenderly back to health.

10

The Metropolitan Museum Buys Boehm Porcelains

I was still working at Meyrowitz when I had one of those totally impossible brainstorms. There had to be *some* way to shorten those hundred years everyone said it would take for Boehm porcelain to become famous. I wanted some glory for Ed and me much sooner than that! Propelled once again by Ed's dictum, "Work only with the best," I went straight to the top: I decided to contact the country's leading authority on porcelain, and I was not going to let the fact that I'd never met him intimidate me.

On my next lunch hour, I dropped a coin into a pay phone on Fifth Avenue and reached Mr. Vincent Andrus, the highly respected curator of the American Wing of the Metropolitan Museum. I could scarcely believe my luck—he answered his own phone!

"Mr. Andrus?" The rest tumbled out in a rush: "I'm Helen Boehm, the wife of Ed Boehm. My husband is the only maker of hard-paste porcelain in America, and we would like you to see the handsome 'Percheron Stallion' and 'Hereford Bull' he's created in our Trenton studio. And we also have a boxer dog, Leghorns, and other fancy fowl."

I paused for breath and suddenly realized I hadn't heard so much as a "Hmm" from him. I shivered in the cold phone booth. Had I gone too far this time? I began to feel a sinking sensation, but then a firm, cultivated voice came across the line: "But, Mrs. Boehm, we don't make hard-paste porcelain in this country."

At least I'd got a response!

I checked my watch. There wasn't much time. I knew Mr. Cook would give me "that look" if I were even a minute late. Mustering a tone almost as firm as his, I countered quickly, "May I show you, please? I think you'll be very surprised and amazed at my husband's accomplishment. We have a very small collection on the second floor of a shop on the corner of Forty-fourth Street and Fifth Avenue."

I was using part of a narrow tailor shop near Meyrowitz as my "Boehm office in New York." In exchange for a porcelain or two, I had arranged to occupy a small space on the second floor rent-free. There, on a folding table covered with a beige satin cloth—a remnant I'd scoured the fabric shops to find—I would set up my porcelain display for prospective buyers.

The tailor shop was the setting for many a drama for me. For one thing, you never knew who would walk in. One day I found myself being introduced by the owner, as a courtesy, to someone who came in regularly to have his suits made. It was Al Capone's right-hand man. He was a friendly type, and within a few days he was confiding to me what a nice man Al Capone was, and wasn't it a shame he was in prison, especially because his wife, "an Italian just like you," wasn't "taking the separation very well." I felt so sorry for her that I sent a little porcelain bird to the gangster's bereft wife. The henchman, in gratitude, declared that if ever I needed a fur coat—or anything else, for that matter—he "had a cousin in the business." When I told him I couldn't possibly afford anything like that, he proudly brought in a secondhand mink as a gift. It was *very* secondhand—not quite long enough, with sleeves that were too short and fur that was slightly discolored. There was no label in it, but I wasn't about to ask where it came from. In spite of its antique air, a mink was still a mink. "This one will give me character, if not importance," I said to myself and hastily put $25 in his hand. I would not accept a *free* coat, however bedraggled, from anyone, least of all from Al Capone's right-hand man. And so I became the proud owner of a fur coat. It was my way of proving to myself that Ed and I were on our way to the top.

I'm still not sure why Mr. Andrus decided to venture down from the world's greatest museum to my little tailor shop. He must have been curious about the person who had dared suggest that an American was making hard-paste porcelain.

On the appointed day, I flew from Meyrowitz to the shop and finished organizing my small display just as Mr. Andrus was due. I scrutinized the elevator indicator, waiting for it to click on my floor.

It was thirty minutes past his appointment, and I was expected back from "lunch" in ten minutes when at last he arrived, a tall elegantly dressed man in a beautifully tailored blue suit and vest. Without a word, he went straight to the display, and I saw his eyes focus on one piece after another. He appeared singularly unimpressed. I crossed my fingers behind my back and said a little prayer.

"Mrs. Boehm," he said, after what I felt was an eternity, "I'd like very much to buy these two pieces," and he pointed to the "Percheron Stallion" and the "Hereford Bull."

"Oh, no, Mr. Andrus!" I blurted out, nearly fainting with relief. "You don't need to buy them, I'll *give* them to you."

"The Metropolitan Museum of Art, Mrs. Boehm, has a budget for acquisitions, and that," he continued, his eyes twinkling, "includes porcelains for the American Wing."

He drew out his pen and wrote a purchase order totaling $60—$30 for each porcelain.

I personally delivered the Stallion and the Hereford to the museum the next day on my lunch hour. I unpacked them myself, afraid that someone else might break the colorful pink roses on the Percheron's mane.

It was only after I left the museum and knew my dream had come true that I told Ed what had happened. I ran to the nearest pay phone. "It's happened, Ed, it's really happened! Your porcelains are in the Metropolitan Museum!"

With this major victory for our tiny Trenton studio, I returned to previously reluctant buyers to relay the news. *Now they listened.* Within a short time, they would all be back to buy.

In the meantime, I decided to make another dream come true

and worked up the courage to call the *New York Times*. A story from them would go a lot further than my legs would in ten years of lunch hours. If the definition of *marketing* is "wanting to get somewhere in a hurry," then I had a talent for it from the start.

The *Times* assigned the late Sanka Knox, their leading art critic, to write an in-depth story on Ed Boehm and his work. That meant Ed had to come in to New York for the interview. It took me four hours to help him overcome his shyness and discomfort at the mere thought of publicity about himself. I used every argument I could think of to convince him of the importance of this interview. He finally agreed to meet Mrs. Knox, but he did so quite reluctantly.

To this day I can quote most of the article by heart. "Boehm," wrote Mrs. Knox, "is a farmer turned artist." She also quoted Mr. Andrus of the Metropolitan Museum, who said, "The realistic ceramics are equal to the finest of superior English work." The story appeared January 20, 1951.

With the prestigious endorsement of the Metropolitan Museum of Art and the major *New York Times* story, the acceptance of Boehm porcelain greatly increased among important collectors and buyers.

Our customers began ordering more pieces. The buyers pressed for a greater variety of subjects. I began to hear questions like "Why doesn't your husband make something other than just cows and bulls? What about flowers? And birds?"

Ed knew his birds, and he knew that in time he could sculpt them. It would be a big change from the solid, massive proportions of cattle and horses, and it was psychologically hard for him to move away from those majestic animals. But he had to listen to what the marketplace was saying.

Together we launched the now world-famous Boehm birds. Ed began with the songbirds. They were an instant success with the galleries and stores, which immediately demanded limited editions for their special customers. By 1956 the business was growing so rapidly that I hired a distributor to free myself for other work. When the distinguished firm of Meakin and Ridgeway, Inc., sales representatives of England's great Minton china, agreed to handle the Boehm line, it was a needed good omen. I could not devote myself totally to both promotion and the day-to-day administrative work at the studio. (I had by that time been able to resign my job at Meyrowitz.)

I began to devise publicity campaigns to promote the porcelains. We had very little money for advertising; I could get more space in the papers through publicity than we ever could afford in buying ad space, so I thought up one scheme after another that might work in a store and be newsworthy. I thought of ideas while dozing on the train, waiting in line at the supermarket, and sitting in airports on weekends. Often only one out of ten ideas were workable, and of those, only one out of ten were considered practical by the retail accounts.

Production soon lagged behind my enthusiastic promotion schemes, and then I realized we had enough to do just in planning ahead for the major public events that would serve as our "targets of opportunity." I closed a straining zipper on my headful of grandiose "get Boehm out in front" schemes—at least temporarily, until production could catch up.

11

The Money Chase

Our financial situation early in 1951 still remained very precarious. Ed and I sat up night after night discussing what to do. With the Metropolitan acquisition and the *New York Times* story in our pockets, we decided it was time for me to take the plunge. I gave Mr. Cook two weeks' notice and left Meyrowitz to work full-time as Ed's business partner and salesperson. Before resigning, I obtained a letter of recommendation from the chairman, Mr. Volt, just in case I had to return to dispensing optics. To this day, I keep my license up to date, partly as insurance, partly for sentimental reasons.

During those years in the early fifties, it seemed to me that I knew all the train conductors and Greyhound drivers who stopped in Trenton, New Jersey. I traveled all over with one small suitcase and several huge boxes of porcelains, which I packed and unpacked carefully myself. No one else could touch the delicate contents. Often I would be on the road twelve or fifteen hours a day, because there was not enough money for me to stay in a hotel.

In fact, the expenses of running a studio had made our backer distinctly nervous. Ed even wondered if he would have to return to cattle breeding and farming. I begged our benefactor to support the studio for just one more month. I would somehow find another backer.

I set off on a trip throughout the South, with Dallas and Houston as the final stops. The guardian angel who always traveled with me told me to take along all the names of everyone in those areas who had ever bought Boehm porcelains.

Sales were slow. After several days I hit my next stop tired and discouraged. I pulled out my list. One man living there had purchased several pieces on a visit to New York. I headed straight for the pay telephone in the train station and called all ten persons listed in the telephone book with the name he'd given. Finally I spoke to a young man who said his father collected "that sort of thing." I pleaded with him to give me his father's office address, then set out to catch my client before he left for lunch.

Burdened by two heavy boxes, I thought my arms would break before reaching his office building. I asked for him and felt a surge of relief as I was shown to his office. A voice boomed out above the sound of a ticker tape clicking away: "So you're the crockery lady!"

A tall, lanky man, my quarry had his feet propped on the desk and was looking at me from behind expensive leather boots. In one hand he held a Coke. He smiled and asked, "What can I do for you, Mrs. Boehm?"

I launched straight into my sales presentation, showing him all the fine points of Ed's beautiful pieces and advising him to buy all the porcelains he could—they might very soon become collectors' items if we had to close down our studio. I wound down my breathless speech by saying I was seeing another tycoon in the same business—whom he might know—in Texas the next day, and would then be heading home. What did he think of these porcelains?

He not only admired the samples of Ed's work, but, as I discovered later, he was bound and determined to outdo the Texas gentleman I had unwittingly mentioned, an influential businessman who happened to be his principal rival. They had crossed swords in a major deal in which the Texas tycoon had bested him. Without so much as batting an eye, he said, "I'll be your partner. Exactly how much do you need?"

And that's how Ed and I obtained the $20,000 we needed to buy out our original backer. Our new backer purchased the firm and gave us a fifty percent interest in it. For us it meant that instead of thirty percent of almost nothing, we now had fifty percent of not much more.

Six months later, in spite of Ed's working around the clock and my crisscrossing the country with untold boxes of porcelain, we still had not managed to make a profit. Understandably, this wouldn't do for a man of our backer's rarin'-to-go temperament, and we received a telegram asking us to resign from the company because he was liquidating it.

Nobody could do something like that to a Franzolin just like that. I picked up the telephone and called his house.

"I'll give you all of our life's savings" I said, "twenty-five hundred dollars, plus all the porcelains in the stockroom at the studio, if you don't pull the rug out from under us and if you sell us your fifty percent of the company."

At that point we had about one hundred pieces, including boxer dogs, race horses, and Angus, Hereford, and Shorthorn cattle. This was an irresistible offer to him. Their value then was perhaps $3,000, but today these pieces are probably worth $100,000. An astute bargainer, he accepted.

It was 1953, just three years after the struggling Boehm porcelain company had started. We didn't have a penny in the bank—we were in debt—but the company was ours, Ed's and mine! We were free—Ed to design, I to market, and both of us to challenge England, Europe, and Asia with the work of Boehm. Somehow we were going to do it all.

Years later, on a trip South in 1971, I repaid our backer for his entire investment in Boehm porcelain. I had told an old collector friend who was looking for some of Ed's early pieces about our backer's unique collection. When he insisted on finding out if it might be for sale, we drove to the man's house to see him. Still wrapped in old Trenton newspapers dated 1953 were the hundred Boehm pieces that had brought us our studio home free. The collector paid our ex-benefactor $27,500 for his early Boehm, and all three of us were happy, especially my good friend the tycoon. His entire investment was returned. I have *always* said no one loses by investing in Boehm porcelain.

Five years ago, that same man, now starting out on a new venture, asked if I would invest in some commodities futures. He needed a financial partner. I did so without hesitation—and without knowing anything about commodities futures—because, although his investment in Boehm had been fully recovered, it was that wonderful *chance* at success that I really had always wanted to give back to him. At last I felt I had said the appropriate "thank you" to him, even though our commodities futures soured and wiped out my substantial investment.

12

The Birds, the Bees, and the Chimpanzees

As soon as we had achieved complete ownership in what is now Edward Marshall Boehm, Inc., our fortunes began to soar. It was as though owning the company outright had been the missing and magical ingredient. Ed's energy seemed to refuel itself. He created more and more exquisite pieces. He was bursting with ideas for new projects. The glazes and colors were working incredibly well, and the orders were coming in strong. I achieved a surprising success with my retail accounts. We were on our way.

In 1954 we purchased the impressive home we had dreamed of for years, with an equally impressive mortgage. It was a handsome Dutch colonial house, in Washington Crossing, New Jersey, overlooking the winding Delaware River. It was a house in which to grow, with incredibly beautiful grounds to nurture. We left our life as spent in miniscule apartments far behind us—except for one thing: We still had birds in our kitchen. We soon had our very own birds outside, too, as Ed began indulging in his passion for collecting exotic birds and fancy fowl. In the next years he built nine aviaries and designed a series of gardens. Our estate became a refuge for any city-weary soul. Visitors could wander from pool to bridge, from bench to grassy knoll, past an Oriental meditation garden, through an English cutting garden, and over to a carefully manicured topiary in the American gardens.

Our place in Washington Crossing was truly the ultimate fantasy world, with its gardens, exotic birds, fancy fowl, monkeys, otters, sea lions, dogs, and an enormous collection of rare tropical fish. When Ed set his mind to something, it engulfed him and he would not be thwarted. One of our friends told me she loved coming to see us because it was like "stepping onto the set of *Dr. Doolittle*" (the movie starring Rex Harrison in which he talked to the animals and they talked back to him). After that, whenever I wandered through the New York Zoological Garden in the Bronx, I wondered why I felt so at home and why it was so familiar. The sounds in the air, minus the roaring of the lions and tigers, were much like the sounds on our place.

Ed's gardens held the same priority as his birds and animals. He first put in the American garden in 1958, then the Japanese garden a year later, and finally the English garden in 1961. For the latter, 240,000 bricks had to be laid, normally a job requiring several months. With his usual impatience, Ed hired twenty bricklayers and worked along with them day and night for two weeks to get the job done. When he began a project, it had to be done the right way, and *fast*.

The aviaries were built in the same manner, all nine of them. They were quonset-shaped, sixty feet long by thirty feet wide and forty feet high. The aviaries and "flights" for the birds extended over four acres, and no scientist ever conducted a lab experiment with more care than Ed did in creating a healthy breeding environment for them. All of the aviaries were constructed to simulate the natural surroundings of their inhabitants at different biotic levels (for birds who stay on the ground, for those who stay mainly at the bush level, and for those who live high in the trees). All of this required a great deal of knowledge, which Ed had, and a lot of money (which we often did *not* have) for air blowers, heating pipes, rock waterfalls, tropical plants, and full-grown trees.

The "Aviary Diary" was a faithfully kept journal in which Ed or the aviary curator wrote a daily comment on the diet and the health of any bird or a note on any plant that needed replacing. The birds were often written about in terms of their personality and character traits. It was important, of course, that only compatible birds be placed in the same aviaries.

No hospital ever had a diet kitchen more thoroughly supervised than Ed's for the aviaries. Each species of bird was fed, usually three times a day, from a numbered pan. The basic soft food mixture was prepared with turkey starter mash, soybean flour, brewers yeast, hard-boiled egg, and grated fresh carrot. Certain birds required a special oil, others bone meal. Some birds required two courses, the second one a kind of fruit cocktail with raisins, diced apples, plantain, and sweet potatoes, with chopped grapes and cherries on alternate days.

When it was necessary to train certain birds to eat in a different manner than in their normal habitat, Ed could manage that, too. The paradise flycatcher, for example, is a voracious insect eater, catching most of its food on the wing. When a shipment of these beautiful birds arrived, Ed spent several days going out to the aviary to feed them every four hours, like an anxious mother tending her newborn. He tossed live mealworms, flies, and crickets in the air for the birds to catch on the wing until he finally trained them to come down to the feeding cups, which contained live food and ground meat. When people called the house asking for Ed during those days, I never summoned the courage to tell them the truth—that Ed was outside, tossing mealworms in the air.

When it was unbearably hot weather, Ed would suddenly rise from his living room chair in the middle of a conversation and leave without explanation. He was going to check on the birds' food, to see if it had dried up or become spoiled in the heat. One night he held our dinner guests mesmerized with his description of the severe feeding problems he was having with the hoopoes. "But I've solved it just this afternoon!" he shouted triumphantly. "I bored the center out of a sweet potato and stuffed it with mealworms. The hoopoes found it delicious!" The guests returned to their roast beef with noticeably diminished enthusiasm, and I was silently grateful that sweet potatoes were not on the night's menu.

The birds were always on Ed's mind, and they were tough competition for me. I wrote a friend that I never had to worry about other women in Ed's life—only about "Lemon-Rumped

Tinker-birds, Double-toothed Barbets, and Bare-Faced Go-Aways."

Ed was justifiably angered and frustrated whenever foreign agents shipped him birds and the fragile creatures arrived dead, so he began trapping his own birds in South America, Australia, and Africa. He went often to the richest bird country in the world, Ecuador. On one trip in Africa he hired white hunters to help him and safely brought back one hundred sixty prized specimens.

That trip was not without incident. On the way home, Ed entered the cargo hold of the plane at every airport stop to feed his birds and clean their cages. When the airliner approached the United States, bad weather in New York forced the plane to land in Boston in a snowstorm. Ed and his aviary curator managed to get the birds into taxis and went to the railroad station to board a train for the five-hour trip to New York. The two men spent the entire train trip with the birds in an unheated baggage car. Ed found some metal wastebaskets in the car and, as usual, had an idea of how to cope with the crisis at hand. He went through the passenger section of the train and asked all the passengers for their discarded newspapers. These he set fire to in the wastebaskets back in the baggage car—naturally without the knowledge of the train crew—thus keeping the temperature high enough to keep the birds alive. This turn of events did not surprise me at all, for this was a man who would drop everything to fix a bird's broken leg or wing. To me it was quite natural that he would risk setting fire to an entire baggage car in order to keep his precious cargo alive.

Occasionally even Ed was forced to abandon his dream of breeding certain species of birds to present to zoos around the world. The red-legged thrush, for example, was inclined to be a bully and to lack any appreciable song. The red-chested cuckoos were avid live-food eaters and were a hazard in the aviary when insectivorous species were breeding. The blue-bearded bee-eaters had to be disposed of because honey bees become angry when disturbed. The people collecting the bees were stung so often that they decided fetching the bee eaters' supper was not worth their own suffering.

Some of the birds were friendly and quite tame, like the

common trumpeters from Ecuador, who would follow workers around like dogs following their masters and trumpet whenever a visitor arrived, usually in unharmonious accompaniment to the barking of the dogs.

The late Sir Edward Halstrom, the famous zoologist who founded and financed the Taronga Zoo in Sydney, Australia, was known internationally as "Mr. Bird of Paradise," because of the many species of exotic birds he bred on his plantations in New Guinea. When he visited Ed's aviaries in 1959 and saw the knowledge and care that went into the breeding programs, he sent Ed a collection of rare birds of paradise as a gift, and from then on, Sir Edward and Ed Boehm exchanged letters, birds, and animals. Ed became a very special friend of Sir Edward's, and even trained animals for the Taronga Park Zoo.

One of these animals was little Lulu, an adorable, saucy baby chimpanzee who became an intimate member of our household. Ed walked into our kitchen one morning bearing a tiny member of the most intelligent species of the animal kingdom and put her into my arms. I held her for a long time. That little face looked up at me with a most bemused, quizzical expression, as if to say, "Well, who are you, if I might ask?" I was not even insulted when Ed, gazing on the scene with admiration, said in a tender tone, "Helen, you look like a mother and child." Coming from someone else, that statement might have been a joke or an insult; coming from Ed, it was a compliment.

I carefully weighed and measured Lulu for clothes, then drove to the local department store in Trenton to purchase a yellow and white layette, a wooden highchair, and an unbreakable porridge set. The sales clerk looked at me with a gushing smile. "Oh, are you the lucky mother?"

"No," I replied quickly.

"Oh, then for a friend's new baby girl?" she asked with equal gushiness.

"No," I replied, "not for a friend's baby. It's for our . . . er . . . chimpanzee."

"Oh, I see," she said. Her face fell like a rubber band that's been stretched and let go. "Oh, I see," she repeated, as if no other words would apply. "How lovely." Fortunately, another customer approached us, carrying a baby—a human one. The sales clerk handed me my receipts and the packages I was able to carry and sped off gratefully in the direction of the *homo sapiens* baby.

Lulu not only had the run of our basement, she also was allowed to live in the kitchen, where Ed trained her to eat and play. She learned how to dial the telephone, how to eat my good spaghetti *alla carbonara*, and how to sit at the table with us at mealtimes.

Thank goodness for Haralene Hood, the wonderful housekeeper we had for thirty years. Not only could she put a splint on a bird's leg, but she could deal with a baby chimp with ease. She changed Lulu's diapers, bathed her, fed her Pablum and milk from a bottle, and washed and ironed her little dresses with the patience of a well-trained nursemaid.

Lulu quickly came to love Ed and followed him everywhere. She clung tightly to his leg, just as a child often does with her daddy's leg or hand. Eventually she grew to maturity and was strong enough to make a sea voyage. Under the watchful eye of the captain, a friend of Sir Edward, she traveled by ship to Australia for her new life in the Taronga Zoo. Ed and I were very sad when we waved good-bye to her, but we knew she would have an enjoyable life with the other chimps in training to perform at that illustrious zoo.

We were not lonely for too long. Soon Chico, the macaw, appeared on the scene at Washington Crossing. He, too, had the run of the kitchen. He wandered around on the linoleum floor, walking pigeon-toed from the table to the refrigerator and back again.

Chico was well behaved, at least most of the time. But after one particularly delicious lunch of juicy fresh blueberries, he took it upon himself to wander into our library—perhaps for a little intellectual diversion—and there, on my beige Oriental rug, he had a large, unfortunate accident.

After that, Chico was "off campus" for a while. He had to live "like a bird" in the aviary until I forgave him and he was reinstated in the Boehm household.

Soon after Chico's arrival, Cocky, a sulphur-crested cockatoo from Australia, joined us. An orphan, Cocky had been nursed in the wild by one of Ed's friends and was well behaved with people. Cocky became *the* pet of the aviary and king of the flock of more than 1500 birds. He chattered with everyone and loved to startle people with, "Hello, stupid, you think you're smart?" Sometimes he would lift his wing and say, "Scratch me."

Cocky's vocabulary often startled people. On one occasion, when Mrs. Davis, wife of the senator from Delaware, traveled from Washington, D. C., to visit, along with other members of the Congressional Club, Ed taught her how to feed the bird his dinner of fruit and seeds. It was a new experience for this very elegant woman. As she was gingerly trying to feed Cocky, the bird suddenly shouted, "Hello, stupid!"

"Cocky," Ed said sternly, "you don't talk to members of Congress or their spouses that way!"

Cocky responded by calling Ed stupid, too, much to the delight of Mrs. Davis.

One day Cocky flew the coop, heading directly across the Delaware River toward the Pennsylvania side. Ed did everything he could to lure him back, but nothing seemed to work, not even putting out his favorite food. After three days, we decided that he was gone forever.

At the end of the week on a warm evening, our neighbors were giving a large cocktail party for their friends in their garden. While everyone was sipping cocktails and eating dainty canapes, one of the guests heard a voice.

"Hello, stupid."

At first the guest ignored the comment, thinking that one of the group had consumed too many glasses of wine. Then Cocky's wild laugh rang out, and our neighbor realized it must be one of Ed's birds making those sounds. He called Ed on the telephone to say that there was "a talking bird in my tree." Ed rushed over with fruit and seeds and slowly coaxed the runaway back into our kitchen, where I was waiting anxiously. The bird looked me in the eye and then screeched, "Scratch me."

"You're not so stupid," I replied. "You knew your way home." The king of the flock had returned. You could sense the relief of the other birds, too, to have Cocky home again.

Anyone passing by earlier that evening who saw Ed luring the bird home, enticing it with fruit as he walked briskly along, might have been greatly puzzled. Ed, in turn, would have been perplexed as to why the passerby was puzzled.

13

White House Magic

As our successes and fortunes grew, so did my responsibilities. Instead of working eight hours a day, I found myself working fourteen hours a day. I was the combination office manager, sales department, and bookkeeper. I was married to a man who had absolutely no head for figures and who, once we were married, never wrote a check for the rest of his life. I paid all the bills and kept the expense ledger. Ed would occasionally pry into the state of our bottom line. If he found it the slightest bit salutary, he would purchase something for our place to put us back in debt.

Money meant absolutely nothing to him. If a prized cow cost $10,000, he'd buy it and ask me later how we would pay for it. He once ordered $20,000 worth of trees and bushes without asking the price, and yet, if I asked him please to buy a new suit, his answer inevitably would be, "Why, Helen, you know we can't afford it just now." One day when I was toiling over our books in the house in Washington Crossing, an enormous truck pulled into our driveway, right outside my window. We had overspent this particular month, and I was making notes on our financial projections. I watched with disbelief as Ed rushed out into the driveway and began helping the driver unload the

68

contents of the truck—enough azalea plants from Alabama to create a forest!

The results of these major expenditures always forced me into fast action. I would go out on the road sooner than planned and would stay out much later than planned. I went to more stores, opened new accounts, and pushed our regular accounts harder to buy more. Somehow a flow of incredible energy would always come, and somehow it always worked. Occasionally a big break would come in the form of someone like Jesse Jones (formerly Secretary of Commerce and head of the Reconstruction Finance Corporation), who purchased six major porcelains. He subsequently donated these to the Houston Museum of Fine Arts as part of his program for preserving important examples of American art. A few months later, the Louisiana State Museum acquired three porcelains, too, and suddenly it seemed that buying Boehm had become very important.

In the early 1950s, it didn't take me long to come to the conclusion that if the Metropolitan Museum of Art wanted Boehm pieces, why not the White House? Of course Ed, typically cautious in marketing matters, thought this time I'd really overreached myself. But the irrepressible optimist in me reasoned that if the Metropolitan's Mr. Andrus was curious enough to come to a tiny little tailor shop to look at porcelains, the White House might be just as curious about our Trenton studio. After all, the Eisenhowers had many fine beef cattle on their Pennsylvania farm. Wouldn't a gift of a porcelain Hereford bull be unexpected enough to interest them?

It would and it did. Two weeks after I wrote Mrs. Eisenhower, in February of 1954, the postman rang my bell. "Mrs. Boehm, you have a letter on White House stationery . . . but there is three cents postage due!" (He has treated me with great respect ever since that day.)

I paid the three cents, opened the letter eagerly, and there was an invitation from Mrs. Eisenhower for lunch, which I happily accepted. I left for Washington in my old 1947 green Buick. As I approached the White House, I just happened to turn on the car radio. The news bulletins were full of frightening reports of people wildly shooting at members of Congress. A newscaster announced that special security precautions were being taken at all major government buildings, including the White House.

I had now reached 1600 Pennsylvania Avenue. Secret Service men were inspecting the one or two cars in front of me. Just as I was about to drive through the famous iron gates, I slammed on my brakes, turned down a side street, and raced out of view of the White House. I had realized there was a rifle in the trunk! On the way down to Washington, I had stopped in Baltimore at Ed's cousin's to pick up a rifle Ed was going to use the following weekend for duck shooting. There it was, right next to the porcelain Hereford bull for Mamie. Under normal circumstances, it would have been difficult enough to pass inspection, but that day!

I parked the car a few blocks from the White House and raced frantically into the street to hail a taxi. It was already the lunch hour, and I didn't need an etiquette book to tell me you don't keep the First Lady waiting. Many taxis, full of passengers, passed me by. Finally one stopped near me to let out its passengers, and I practically commandeered it. We arrived at 1600 Pennsylvania, the northwest gate, only five minutes after I was due.

The White House police checked my ID and lifted the porcelain sculpture from the box to inspect it while I died a thousand deaths for fear they would break it. They then sent me up the curving drive to the North Portico, past the West Wing, where White House press members were rushing through the doors to a news session with the president's press secretary. I could not believe this was me, carrying my box, climbing the stairs leading to the shiny doors of the president's house. The chief usher, J. B. West, stepped out to greet me. "Welcome to the White House, Mrs. Boehm," he said, and a footman dressed in a club coat and morning trousers appeared from behind him and whisked my box from my arms. I followed Mr. West across the inlaid marble floor of the great front hall, our footsteps echoing loudly. As we walked, I turned to the left and right, catching every glimpse I could of the house. To the left I saw the East Room with its heavy crystal chandeliers, the rich gold damask draperies, and the parquet floors shining mirror-bright. Ahead of us was the Blue Room with its round table in the center holding a mammoth arrangement of flowers, and beyond it, through the French doors, was the broad sweep of the south lawns and the Washington Monument and the Jefferson Memorial. I felt awe-struck. There was no one around except footmen, dressed in black tie, busy cleaning and polishing. To the right of us was the State Dining Room with its great silver-gilt service on a tray in the center of the massive dining table.

I had lunch alone with Mrs. Eisenhower, an hour of magic in my life. We dined on consommé and roast chicken tarragon at a small table that had been set up in the Red Room. There were large portraits of former presidents hanging on the crimson red fabric-covered walls. I remember the graceful white marble fireplace with vermeil urns and a marble and bronze French clock. Mrs. Eisenhower was natural, gracious, a real person who immediately put me at ease. The president at one point put his head in the door to say hello, and I handed him the sculpture of the Hereford bull. His eyes lit up when he saw it, and he told me to congratulate Ed on his artistry. With that famous Eisenhower grin, the president looked like a young boy standing there in the doorway of the Red Room, affectionately patting the flanks of the Boehm porcelain bull.

I kept thinking about Papa, that he must be watching this from his place in heaven. I would describe every second of this hour later to Ed, but I wanted the Franzolins up there— wherever heaven is—to know that Helen had made it to the White House.

This was also the beginning of a long friendship between the Eisenhowers and the Boehms. We shared common interests in cattle and farming, as well as in art. Eventually Ed purchased one of Ike's prized Angus cows, named Black Jestress. He named one of its offspring Duncravin Mamie, after his favorite First Lady.

As for me, I made it a rule never again to drive to the White House with a gun in the car trunk.

14

A Time for Twins

At one point in our lives, Ed and I were surrogate parents. My sister shared her twin girls with us for four exciting years, 1954 to 1958. My two nieces, Francene and Teresa D'Antona, the daughters of my eldest sister, Michaela, lived with us from the ages of fourteen to eighteen during their years of high school at the Villa Victoria Academy in Trenton.

It was not always an easy life for the girls, because Ed was a strict disciplinarian, and their school friends had much freer lives. He wanted them to be perfect and, of course, there is no such thing as the perfect child—or a perfect adult, for that matter. We had sad times as well as joyful times together. Francene recalls vividly how her uncle taught her self-discipline from the very first day. He spent more time with the twins than I did, because I was on the road so often. It became Ed's responsibility by default to set the rules by which the girls had to abide, just as my father had done for my sisters and me many years before.

Ed planned their leisure time, sometimes not in the most conventional of ways. One day he said to Francene, then fifteen, "Since I can't use my ticket for a boxing match, I dare you to go to Yankee Stadium in the Bronx tonight to see the fight between

Sugar Ray Robinson and Carmen Basilio. As a matter of fact, I'll give you fifty dollars if you do it!"

At first Francene was afraid. After all, it was not easy or even safe for a young teenager to go alone from Trenton to the Bronx. She was not used to the city, but she accepted the challenge her uncle had offered her. Attending the fight would be much more fun than doing her French homework! She went through the evening with butterflies in her stomach, feeling extremely proud of herself. "Actually, Aunt Helen," she told me later, "everyone looked at me as though I was someone's daughter whose parents were right close to me. No one even realized I was alone." A kind couple she met during the evening saw that she boarded the right train back to Trenton. Ed had not even foreseen that she might have trouble coming home alone.

Ed thought it was important for the girls to "try their wings," but when I returned home from my selling trip and heard about the prize-fight incident, I was furious. Ed and I never resolved our differences over the meaning of an education. To me, it was staying home and doing one's French homework; to him, it was savoring life's adventures and learning how to take care of oneself in all situations.

Every other weekend the twins went home to their mother and father, who lived in Valley Stream, Long Island. They would sneak a hamster or Lee Lee, Francene's favorite miniature schnauzer, onto the train, wrapped like a baby in swaddling clothes. The conductors naturally knew that this was no baby under the pink covers, but they just looked the other way.

Lee Lee was also the cause of a continuing disagreement between Francene and Teresa. Uncle Ed taught Francene to handstrip and trim her dog and make her ready for any dog show. After Francene had finished the hours of hard work grooming Lee Lee, Teresa would primp, put on high heels, attach a fancy lead to Lee Lee's rhinestone collar, and parade her up and down the neighborhood as though she had done all the grooming work. This habit infuriated Francene and her Uncle Ed equally.

The twins had chores to do each day, and their uncle tolerated no excuses, no laziness. On school days, they rose very early in the morning in order to exercise and water the fifty or sixty dogs in the kennels, a task that required well over an hour. When they returned home from classes, before anything else, even homework, they had to clean the kennels very thoroughly and dish out a special mixture of food to the dogs. Often Ed would inspect to see that they had done a proper job. He did not care about the menu or dinner table for his human guests, but he certainly cared about how his animals were fed.

Francene remembers the times they all piled into a car and drove to a dog or horse show. Uncle Ed would also take them to a zoo and teach them wonderful things about the animals—"an education," Francene says, "we never could have received at any school."

Francene recalls "the time Uncle Ed had us planting tulip bulbs—at midnight. We had begun the task late in the afternoon after cleaning the kennels. There were at least two hundred bulbs, and he wanted them all in the ground on *that* day, not the next. He was getting the garden all beautiful for Aunt Helen, who was returning from a trip later that week.

"My sister and I thought we'd be able to get out of doing the planting once it turned dark, so we dawdled along a little bit. But no, that didn't work. Uncle Ed gave each of us a high-powered flashlight after dinner and told us to keep on until we finished.

"We actually loved it, though, because we felt important and needed. We felt we were helping the grownups. Our lives were very different from those of our friends. We learned much more than the other girls growing up in 'regular' families. At times the strictness really got to us, but we were actually the envy of our classmates."

There is no question but that Ed was a tough taskmaster, especially while I was away. Sometimes I had to go in the other direction to compensate for the arduous regimen he wanted them to follow. One thing they knew, however, was that he loved them very much.

When they began to date, Ed was not very happy. He was so attached to "his girls" that he didn't want to share their leisure time with any young men. When their beaux were around, he would make so much noise in the room where they were gathered that there was little time for normal socializing. When the girls complained, Ed would retort, "There's plenty of time for romance in the future!"

But the twins were attractive and popular. Ed failed to discourage the suitors permanently, and he lived to see both girls happily married. Today, each has two children. Francene has two girls: Lenore, age nineteen, and Christine, twelve. Teresa has boys: Carl, sixteen, and Edward, thirteen.

It pleases me to see my nieces grown into womanhood, leaders in their communities and involved in many artistic and charitable projects. I am sure their tough teacher, Ed Boehm, was responsible for a good part of their character, because he influenced them greatly during the important years of their adolescence.

15

The Great Tiffany Bird Escape

Ever since Ed had made his first porcelain animal, I had felt that Tiffany's, the Fifth Avenue jeweler, was the ultimate success symbol. I used to walk up and down past the clever theatrical set windows Gene Moore did for Tiffany's, absorbing the design of the jewels and the design genius of Moore in his placement of them. I longed to go in there and have someone in one of those forbidding fifth-floor executive offices say, "Why, of course, Mrs. Boehm, we would be glad to carry Boehm porcelain."

They keep calling it "the luck of the Irish." I call it the "luck of the Italians." One day I summoned my courage to call on the head of the Bonwit Teller gift department on the second floor. (Bonwit's was next door to Tiffany.) To my surprise I found out it was Pauline Hoving, wife of Walter Hoving, the chairman of both Bonwit's and of Tiffany's.

Pauline Hoving had made a tremendous success of her gift shop. She shopped all around the world, and other "taste-makers" in New York routinely dropped by to see her newly arrived merchandise. She was a trend setter; people copied her.

I opened all of the boxes I had brought with me and put the porcelain figurines on her desk. She picked them up and began to discuss the art of porcelain. Her knowledgability about the

76

Chinese porcelain and her comments on the interlocking parts and many technical aspects of Ed's work left me stunned. She finally looked at me with her formidable, rather cold eyes and said, "I'd like to help you, Mrs. Boehm. I think this work is excellent." Then she picked up Ed's painted Canada geese group and said, "Take off the decoration. Have your husband do these in all-white bisque. It would be very chic." I thought to myself how dull looking they would be without color—lifeless, in fact. But I brought the idea home to Ed. He made a pair of them, working rather unenthusiastically—until he saw them finished. They were stunning. The white bisque Canada geese were subsequently the subject of a Bonwit ad on page three of the *New Yorker*.

We were made by that. Bonwit's subsequently took other animals and birds and our whole new line of baby birds. Pauline Hoving remarked, "We had all the babies lined up, and they all just 'flew away,' instantly sold." She continued to advise us on what directions to follow. I admired her more than I can possibly say, because of her great taste and because her instincts were accurate and her knowledge profound, not only of art but of *what would sell*.

Her husband, Walter Hoving, kept hearing about the Boehm figurines as he watched the sales sheet at Bonwit's gift department rising steadily. Finally he called me into his office at Tiffany's, and the dream Ed and I had always had materialized. Tiffany's began to carry Boehm porcelain.

I also landed the Ackermann Gallery on East Fifty-seventh Street, one of the most prestigious names in the field of antiques. Along with the account I already had with Black Starr & Gorham, we had New York covered in just the manner it ought to be.

Success! How sweet it does smell!

Tiffany's, as everyone knows, is a very sedate place where everyone behaves well, in a manner befitting a building sitting on the world's most expensive piece of real estate and containing millions of dollars in inventory in jewels, silver, crystal, and china. It is not the kind of place where one expects to find exotic birds flying around loose in a frenzy matched only by that of the employees and customers attempting to catch them.

In 1957, Tish Baldrige was Tiffany's first public relations director. She and I sat and planned a very unusual exhibit for the china and glasswares floor of the store. It was to be a major exhibition of Boehm porcelain birds, and the more we talked, the more excited we both became. Ed's new collection of birds to be unveiled at this exhibit was extraordinarily beautiful; this show must be worthy of his work.

Ed by this time had installed in the gardens of our New Jersey home a large temperature-controlled aviary to house his collection of exotic birds from all over the world.

"Tish," I said suddenly, "I have a great idea. I'll bring in some of Ed's live birds to make the exhibit of his porcelain ones even more exciting!"

"Great!" Tish answered. "Now where will we put them? We can't have them flying around the store."

We both laughed at such a non-Tiffany image, little realizing that this preposterous scene would later actually be played out.

I had a solution of how to house the live birds. I recalled seeing a lovely Spanish antique wire bird cage in New Orleans, so I called an old friend there. He very generously dispatched it to me at once as a gift.

Almost six feet high, the Victorian painted cage looked like a quaint gazebo. It could hold about twenty birds as long as they were, as Ed described it, "harmonious." The cage had a gallery all around the bottom, so the birds would not mess up Tiffany's richly carpeted floor.

Ed, who never wanted to part with a live bird or an animal for any reason, reluctantly agreed to "loan" some of his live birds for the exhibition. I promised to handle them personally so no harm could befall them.

On a rainy, cold Columbus Day, Ed loaded the station wagon with a wide selection of exotic birds. He did not look at all pleased to see his prized specimens locked into crude little carrying cages. He himself had netted some of them in South America, Africa, Ecuador, and New Guinea. Some of them were beef eaters, some seed and fruit eaters, and one or two dined only on sweet nectar.

The locks on two of the cages had not been securely fastened. As I drove across Manhattan that morning, the car went over a number of potholes and, unnoticed by me, the doors of those two cages became unhooked. I parked on Fifty-seventh Street at the side entrance of Tiffany's in order to unload the birds, and as I opened the rear of the station wagon, the birds in those cages flew out and soared up to the sky!

I leapt about madly trying to catch them, to grab them by their tails. But they flew higher and higher, swirling pinwheels of color receding into the cold dampness of Fifth Avenue. I called Tish in her office. She rushed down, and together we spread the alarm to passersby, doormen, and policemen to be on the lookout for the little birds. We placed the other fifteen birds safely in the big Victorian cage, and I went to call Ed with the bad news.

A crowd was already waiting in front of the big bronze Tiffany doors, beneath the store's famous clock. The morning papers had carried an ad announcing the Boehm porcelain exhibition including the live birds.

Ed's response was unrepeatable. I pleaded with him to send five more birds into New York to substitute for the missing ones. He agreed, but only after I promised in blood to watch them every second. The local police precinct by now had officially reported "missing birds at Tiffany's." And a reporter who was hanging around the precinct waiting for a story jumped on it. Immediately it became an item on television and radio newscasts, and soon the press was on top of us.

That night, I appeared on television, and by now "The Big Bird Hunt of Manhattan" was a national story. I told Johnny Carson, who was host on the "Tonight Show" (in place of Jack Paar), how rare and valuable Ed's birds were and how it had taken him many, many years to collect the more exotic ones. I also gave the public detailed instructions on how to care for and feed them just in case someone watching the show happened to find one of them.

By now the Tiffany switchboard was completely tied up with incoming calls. Calls came from New Jerseyites, New Yorkers, Long Islanders, and people in Fairfield County, all of whom thought they had seen one or more of the birds. One of the calls actually seemed to merit serious investigation: Two longshore-men told Tish they'd captured three of the Boehm birds at Pier 61 in Brooklyn. They apparently had landed there during the early hours of morning and now were safely stowed away in a huge carton.

Tish immediately dispatched a special messenger down to the waterfront, but he came back empty-handed. When I asked why, he explained laughingly that the box had contained pigeons and grackles, nothing even remotely resembling Ed's exotic specimens.

In the meantime, children, shoppers, and business executives were pouring into Tiffany's, carrying dead birds in paper bags, including tiny sparrows wrapped in tinfoil.

After identifying their birds, Tish and I gave each person a blue Tiffany box in which to bury them if they wished, or else we offered to take care of the problem. Of course, none of Ed's precious birds was found. Walter Hoving, a man who felt that sales should have top priority during every minute the big doors were open in the store, was beside himself while the traffic of dead-bird carriers poured in and out of his emporium and tied up his telephone lines.

This was not the end of the bird episode. Gabe Pressman, a reporter from NBC-TV, arrived with his crew to film the Boehm bird exhibit and hear me tell the story of the five missing whydahs.

In the meantime, Tish had obtained a record album of songbirds, to lend some additional bird ambiance to our exhibit. While Gabe began to interview me, she played the record softly. The birds in the cage did not know about such things as records; they thought the songs and calls came from real birds nearby. What none of us knew was that in the middle of the record a screech owl, an enemy of small birds, was heard, which caused the birds to panic and fly around frantically in the cage, trying to escape. Three of them managed somehow to squeeze through the narrow wires of the cage and escape to the freedom of Tiffany's vast china and glasswares department. They flew into the mirrored columns, swooped around the crystal chandeliers, fluttered over porcelain figurines, fragile goblets, and $1000-a-plate china services. It was pandemonium. Gabe Pressman and his cameramen got it all. I soon forgot about them, however. The customers joined the salespeople in trying to catch the terrified birds. When Walter Hoving arrived on the floor and surveyed the melée of people and frightened birds, he looked as though he could cheerfully have administered poison to me on the spot.

"Helen, what are you doing? Get those birds out of here!"

"Tish!" he then barked at his public relations director. "You and your promotions! I don't care what you do, but do it *fast!*" No one knew what to do—none of us had exactly had training in bird-catching. Customers were ducking the circling birds and batting at them with their handbags. "Ed," I thought to myself, "why aren't you here when I need you?" When I called him at home, he was not there. Tish called the ASPCA, but they were closed because it was Columbus Day. Finally, we had a brainstorm and we reached a pet store that was open. They suggested we wait until it got dark, about five o'clock, and then turn off all the lights one by one. I put some bird food in a bowl and two of us held flashlights. The birds came toward the last rays of light, and we caught them with men's handkerchiefs. It took us over two hours to corral the birds and place them back in their antique cage. The birds must have been as happy as we were that it was all over. I looked at Tish and Tish at me, and we started to laugh and didn't stop for a very long time.

More than five thousand people came into the store that week to see the birds in the cage, probably hoping there would be more escapes. We made headlines in six hundred newspapers— not only in America but in Japan, Germany, and elsewhere. The NBC-TV shots of the birds escaping inside Tiffany's were shown around the world. It made a wonderful story, but it took many weeks before Ed forgave me for losing five of his precious rare birds. It took Walter Hoving longer than that to forgive Tish and me. Because of the confusion, no sales had been made on the china and glasswares floor for that entire afternoon.

It was very ironic that on the same day another animal escape took place at the very same time on the West Side. A Brahma bull somehow managed to run away from the rodeo being held at

Madison Square Garden. The frightened animal made its way up Broadway, stopping traffic for miles, until it was finally lassoed by a quick-moving cowboy on a horse.

The next morning's papers featured stories headlined: "Birds and Bull Startle New York," "New York People Learn About the Birds and Bull," "Birds and Bull Fly the Coop in Gotham," and other similarly amusing lines.

Twenty-five years later, in 1981, we would have a similar event involving live birds and porcelain birds, but with a different purpose: to call attention to the cruel indifference among the majority of humans to the plight and disappearance of certain species of our feathered friends.

When our studios were finishing making an incredibly lifelike peregrine falcon, a greatly endangered species, I picked up the newspaper and read that Donald Fordyce, the young president of Manhattan Life Insurance Company, had reported a miracle on the roof of his Fifty-seventh Street building in mid-Manhattan. A peregrine falcon family had come there to roost. Since none had been sighted in New York for many years, this was a great story. It meant the possibility that the family would hatch its young and that perhaps the peregrine falcon would become less endangered.

We told Mr. Fordyce about our own falcon, and he immediately purchased one to place in his executive office reception room to commemorate the miracle of nature in progress on his roof. We had a little ceremony for the press, because New Yorkers love any kind of nature story. A fierce-looking live peregrine falcon sat on his perch in the reception area (not one of the family on the roof, which could not be disturbed, but a captured falcon, accompanied by his own handler). Our porcelain peregrine falcon was put on a pedestal and covered with a shroud, right next to the live one. At the crucial moment in the press conference, the Boehm falcon was unveiled, and the crowd in attendance gasped. It was the exact same size and had the exact coloration, expression, everything of the live one on the perch next to it. A carbon copy! The live falcon first stared at it (with what looked like unmitigated surprise and disbelief) and then began to take it seriously. He pecked at the porcelain feathers, flapped his wings, and finally began a mating call! Then, frustrated, he began making a distress call.

The entire group gathered there erupted in laughter. The noisy spectacle continued only for a few seconds, because we realized that in deference to the live peregrine falcon, we should remove his porcelain twin brother. The live one stared at the porcelain one as it was taken out of the room. He was one unhappy and very puzzled falcon.

16

Papa Giovanni

With just a little help from God, Boehm porcelain traveled across the Atlantic to Italy and the Vatican three times. The first trip was made in 1959, when the head of the Catholic church was the very popular Pope John XXIII.

It all began because of a request from Monsignor Emilio A. Cardelia of St. Joachim's in Trenton.

He told me he was going to visit the Pope early in 1959 and he "hinted" that he wanted very much to be able to take "something both beautiful and unusual to His Holiness" as a gift from his parishioners. Monsignor Cardelia had in mind a crucifix in the style of the famous Italian painter Guido Reni.

Ed agreed enthusiastically to the idea but on one condition: that he be allowed to make a realistic, not a stylized crucifix. He used a model in sculpting the figure of Christ and spent many days working to attain anatomical realism.

The corpus was done in white bisque and the cross in black ebony, and the combination made an emotional, inspiring work of art. When Ed finished it, I looked at it and felt deeply moved because my husband had created something in the tradition of great Renaissance art. I knew the Pope would be pleased.

I decided to add something of my own for the Holy Father in the package destined for Rome, so I included one of Ed's lovely bird and flower sculptures, "Cerulean Warblers with Wild Roses." Monsignor Cardelia made the presentations of both pieces in March of that year.

As a result, we were invited to a private audience with His Holiness so he could thank us in person. Ed was on a live-bird-trapping safari in Africa when the invitation came. He was just finishing the job of collecting 160 rare birds, so he arranged to have them sent back to Trenton, then he packed up his equipment and proceeded to Rome to meet me. He did not have the proper clothes with him, having been on safari, so we quickly made some purchases, starting with a dark suit, white dress shirt, and tie. As for me, I knew I had to wear a black dress. I chose one by the designer Fabiani that was cut in the latest silhouette. It unfortunately had a harem hemline, which meant that the dress billowed out over the hips like a parachute, but narrowed tightly at the knees.

After kissing Pope John's ring, I looked up at the cherubic, smiling face and suddenly became aware of his warmth and sweetness as well as his piety. He was indeed a "Pope of the people." Ed stood next to me as I spoke for us both in Italian, genuflecting to show my respect: *"Sua santità, siamo tutti due commossi."* ("Your Holiness, we are both very moved.")

The next thing I knew, I was lying flat on the marble floor, right at His Holiness's feet! The tight harem hemline had not accommodated my genuflection.

I was absolutely mortified. So was Ed. I glanced at his face as I awkwardly rose, the Pope holding one hand for support, Ed the other. I then saw the Pope examining my impossible ballooning skirt with great amusement. He kept saying consolingly, *"Ma non è niente, niente."* ("It is nothing.")

After I regained as much composure as I could muster, His Holiness and I continued conversing in Italian. I explained to him what joy Ed had felt in creating both the crucifix, a religious work, and the "Cerulean Warblers," a work that also had a religious significance, in that any bird is "one of God's creatures."

"These birds are incredible! They look as though they are ready to fly!" the Pope exclaimed. Then he added that my husband's hands were a *"dono di Dio"* (a gift from God).

I tried to explain to the Pope that Ed had been a farmer, but I couldn't remember the word for *farmer*. I turned to the Pope's official interpreter for help, but he was not about to rescue me, as he was apparently annoyed at my speaking Italian when he had wanted to do his job as chief translator.

Finally, after what seemed like an interminable length of time, the interpreter relented. "You mean *contadino* or 'man of the field.' " I thanked him and explained to the head of the Roman Catholic Church that my husband was a *"contadino* turned artist." This Pope had come from a family of farmers, too. He looked once again at Ed's hands and at the two sculptures, and then beaming that familiar cherubic smile, "Papa Giovanni" gave us his special blessing and departed.

It was a very special day for Ed and me.

17

A Presidential Gift to the Royals

I learned at an early age that you don't sniff at a target of opportunity. You not only seize it, you jump on it and ride it right through the home stretch. Ed and I had to live by our wits as well as by his talent and my sales efforts. Wits and targets of opportunity are closely allied in life.

Early in our marriage we used to watch polo at Westbury, Long Island. We found the sport thrilling and absolutely beautiful to observe. Ed would sit watching the horses in action while talking to Paul Brown, the much-loved animal artist, whose calendars were world famous. Ed had, of course, watched the great Herbert Hazeltine in action, too, sculpting Man O' War.

In 1957 it was announced that Queen Elizabeth and Prince Philip were coming to our country, their first trip here since their marriage. I knew President and Mrs. Eisenhower would be looking for a state gift. I knew Prince Philip loved polo more than anything else, and I knew something else: that Edward Marshall Boehm could rise to the challenge of sculpting Prince Philip in porcelain, in action on his horse.

I wrote Mrs. Eisenhower a letter about my idea, and she responded by asking for a sketch from Ed. He worked on it from the minute the letter arrived one morning until three the next morning. We mailed it and for weeks after could scarcely attend

87

to normal business, we were so anxious for news from the White House. Each day that passed without a reply might signal the rejection of our proposal.

Then early on a Tuesday morning, nearly a month later, there was a call from the White House. I called Ed to the telephone and stood there watching his face, grabbing his free hand in both of mine, squeezing until it must have hurt.

"Yes, yes. No, I can get it done by then. That's no problem."

My artist husband's sketch had been selected by President Eisenhower. The recognition we had slaved for was finally at hand. It would mean national—no, *international*—recognition.

Ed and his staff were given four months in which to make the now famous sculpture, "The Polo Player," with its 268 interlocking mold sections.

The day after the presentation of the sculpture to the British royal couple, we were awakened at 6 A.M. by the ringing of the telephone. It was an old friend who ignored my sleep-drugged voice.

"Helen! Run out at once and get today's *New York Times*. Ed's 'Polo Player' is on the front page!"

And indeed the photograph was there at the top of the front page, alongside a photograph of the painting President Eisenhower had done as his gift for Queen Elizabeth and Prince Philip. I picked up the paper at our kitchen door, read the story, and raced all over the house in my nightgown, jumping and shouting like someone who has just won the state lottery. Ed, of course, was immensely pleased and proud, but he took the news much more calmly than I did. In fact, he rolled over and went back to sleep, ignoring my telephone calls to friends and family all over the United States.

Two days later, at NBC's invitation, I took the one existing copy of the "Polo Player" to the "Today Show" studios at Rockefeller Center, where I'd be interviewed by the show's host, Dave Garroway. In Trenton, we packed the delicate sculpture in a crate filled with gallons of popped popcorn enclosed in plastic bags to cushion the statue during its trip to the TV studios. While unpacking it in the studio, some of the plastic bags burst, spewing their contents all over the floor. In spite of a frantic sweep-up, popcorn was scattered all over the slick concrete floor, and during the rest of the entire program the listening audience could clearly hear a snapping, crunching sound as people and camera equipment moved around the studio. The name of Ed Boehm was beamed into millions of homes that morning in the midst of constant crackling sounds. The engineers in the control room were obviously upset, but one later regained his sense of humor and quipped that the "Today Show" should now easily find themselves a popcorn sponsor.

This was not the last to be heard from the "Polo Player." He came back into my life again. While chatting with Lord Mountbatten at a United World College meeting in New York several years later, His Lordship mentioned he had seen the sculpture of Prince Philip on his polo pony in the private quarters of Buckingham Palace.

"I only hope you thought it was an impressive piece," I said none too coyly, waiting for a rush of flattering comments.

"There is something quite wrong with it," he replied dryly.

"Oh?" My heart sank. "What's wrong with it?"

"The prince is shown wearing a white helmet. He never wears white."

I flashed back to the research we had done on the prince before making that sculpture. I had obtained a photograph of Prince Philip playing polo from the British Consulate in New York, and he was *indeed* wearing a white helmet in the photograph. I was not about to argue with Lord Mountbatten, however.

"I would like to write to the palace and offer to correct the piece, if you think I might be able to do that," I said hesitantly.

"Write at once," Lord Mountbatten replied. "I think that's a splendid idea."

In July of 1973 Frank Cosentino, president of our Boehm studios, and I visited Buckingham Palace and retrieved the sculpture from the queen's sitting room.

Correcting the piece after sixteen years was a hazardous task in that the sculpture once again had to be exposed to the high heat of the kilns in order to permanently anneal the new blue color to the helmet. Had it not been for the fact that I had the only replica of the sculpture in my home, I probably wouldn't have risked the firing. I was prepared to give up my piece if something happened to Her Majesty's sculpture in the refiring.

Fortunately, the piece fired successfully, and on my return to London, I personally placed the corrected polo player sculpture in the queen's sitting room.

A reporter got wind of this dramatic happening and wrote a front-page story in the *Worcester Evening News*. The article headline ran, "A Tempest Over the Colour of Prince Philip's Polo Hat Settled with a Paint Brush." The reporter, however, had done his own research as well and noted that I wasn't entirely wrong. Prince Philip had indeed worn a white helmet— *once,* when playing polo in Malta, and that was the photograph we had used.

18

From Princeton Quarterback to President of Boehm

Today I am fortunate to have a very highly skilled staff as well as a very advanced computer system to help manage my company. I also have a crackerjack executive secretary, Dorothy Kay, who keeps my busy international life on track.

When Ed and I began the business, we had only ourselves. I was soon overextended, since I was responsible for the book-keeping, billing, packing, and sales. I was also the office typist-clerk. All of these chores had to be sandwiched into the time that I wasn't out on the road selling. We tried adding some office staff, but there was no one who worked hard, appreciated the art of porcelain, and also had great intelligence. We did not have time to train anyone who was not very quick; we also could not tolerate anyone who handled the porcelains with anything but the greatest care.

Only someone really desperate would have had the gall to call the Princeton University Student Employment Office. I was that desperate, however, and I had that much gall.

"I want a liberal arts graduate who can take shorthand and type well," I said calmly, as though my request were the most natural one in the world.

The voice on the other end was frigid with disapproval.

91

"Mrs. Boehm, we do not emphasize typing and shorthand at Princeton," replied Mr. Wallace, the placement director.

Undaunted, I continued, "And I must have a strong *man*, too, because he will have to carry heavy suitcases filled with porcelains. He must have strong administrative qualities, too, because I need an assistant."

By now the voice on the other end was polite but totally disbelieving. "I'll submit your request, Mrs. Boehm, but I would imagine that your chances of getting one of our graduates are exceedingly slim."

Three weeks later a call came. Ed answered the telephone in our kitchen and shouted at me upstairs. "Helen, it's a Mr. Wallace from Princeton. They say they have a first-string quarterback who can type! Now that is ridiculous. Please take this call. The man who's calling must be nuts."

I picked up the receiver and heard Mr. Wallace say, "Mrs. Boehm, I never thought I would have reason to call you again, but miraculously enough, we have a superior student named Frank Cosentino, a star athlete who wants your job. He graduated in 1956 in the first quarter of his class. He was a liberal arts major; he's twenty-three and has just returned from service in Korea, where he was in the adjutant general's office, involved in briefings for court martial cases. He has also"—the voice now assumed an almost reverent tone—"taken a rush course in typing and shorthand. He can type ninety words a minute!"

"Mr. Wallace, have him come to see us *today*."

When Frank walked into our office at the studio in Trenton, Ed and I were prepared to find a million flaws, because we knew that the combination supposedly inherent in this young man was an impossible one. He was good-looking—dark-eyed and with broad shoulders and the beautiful build of an athlete. I looked him over and decided he at least filled one of the qualifications. He would certainly be able to carry those heavy cases. I tested him on his knowledge of art; he had a good grounding in art history. So far so good. I was sure he would never pass the typing and shorthand, if only because he had passed everything else.

I had been trying to answer a letter to a customer all morning long, so I pulled it out of my typewriter and handed it to him. In less than five minutes he had rewritten it and placed it on my desk, neatly typed and perfectly spaced. In rereading it, I noticed that he had improved the wording and content, even the grammar. I handed the letter to Ed, and he quickly glanced at me, nodding his approval.

The next morning I called Frank Cosentino from the drafty train station platform in Trenton as I was waiting for the 7:30 train to New York.

"Mr. Cosentino," I said, "this is Mrs. Boehm. We want you to join our company." I had called just in time, because Frank had received a good offer from Lipton Tea and had decided to accept it if the Boehm offer did not come through.

Frank Cosentino, at first affectionately referred to by our Boehm workers as "the quarterback secretary," has now been with us for twenty-five years. From the very first he pitched in. He did all the dirty work he was asked to do but also assumed more and more responsibility. Ed was by now totally involved in the artistic side of our operation, while I was totally involved in the increasingly pressured task of selling. The complicated administrative side of our growing business obviously required the attention of a manager like Frank.

He also became a great friend of Ed's. They were colleagues and sports buddies; both were outdoorsmen. Ed never felt comfortable around men who were effete, but there was nothing at all effete about Frank.

Ed liked to win, but in some sports he could not beat Frank. After they had played golf together twice, Ed broke one of his clubs over his knee in frustration on the eighth hole, swearing he would never again challenge his colleague on the golf course. Frank had been playing golf since he was nine. He had caddied all through high school at several private clubs in Rockland County in order to raise money for college. He was an honors student and star athlete in high school and won a scholarship to Princeton.

From the first, it was apparent that Frank was to be much more than a secretary-clerk. By the end of the first year, he had assumed many senior management responsibilities. An expert manager of time, he was able to write four scholarly books in his spare time. The first was *Boehm's Birds—The Porcelain Art of Edward Marshall Boehm*; the next was *Edward Marshall Boehm*

1913–1969. Then came *The Boehm Journey to Ching-te-Chen, China, Birthplace of Porcelain;* and finally, *The Boehm Journey to Egypt, Land of Tutankhamen.* I have often wondered at the dichotomy in Frank Cosentino, an athlete who writes well and loves art.

My luck did not hold when I lost my husband at an early age, but "the luck of the Italians," which I have always contended is stronger than that of the Irish, brought me Frank Cosentino. There is no possible way to measure the value of his strength and support. Frank, who is divorced, and his beautiful daughter, Laura, who lives with him, are very special friends today.

I only hope the job placement office at Princeton realizes what they did for me when they posted a job offering for "someone with a liberal arts education who also can type, take shorthand, and lift heavy objects." Neither the job placement office nor I could have envisaged what the future would bring to the young Princeton graduate: the presidency of the Boehm Company at a very young age.

My mother and father, Francesca and Pietro Franzolin, with my oldest brother, Louis, and sister Michaela, after they emigrated from Genoa in 1911. Mama is pregnant again, this time with Mary.

At fourteen I graduated from junior high school in my Helen Franzolin-designed dress, which won first prize.

Seventeen and showing off in my first party dress, which I designed and made myself

Dr. Gillis with his uniformed receptionist, a recent graduate of New Utrecht High School

Our wedding day—October 29, 1944, at St. Mary's Roman Catholic Church in Bensonhurst, Brooklyn. Ed almost didn't make it, but this photograph proves he did.

Morning breakfast at home in Washington Crossing, New Jersey, with Lulu.

Lulu clings to Ed's leg. Lulu's shoes are in better condition than Ed's.

Ed with a young friend in the Japanese garden of our Washington Crossing estate. I dressed in Japanese attire, too, for this photograph.

Ed in the Indian garden he designed at Washington Crossing

Three cheers for the Boehm Team! From left: Billy Ylvisaker, Alfons Pieres, me, Gonzalo Tanoira, and Bill Ylvisaker, Sr., in Palm Beach in 1982.

Three of my team's 1983 victories. *From left:* the Rothman Trophy won at Windsor Great Park; the Texaco International Trophy won at Cowdray Park; and the eighty-five-year-old Warwickshire Cup won at Cirencester.

At Windsor Great Park with Her Majesty Queen Elizabeth and my victorious team. We had just defeated Les Diables Bleus, including Prince Charles *(third from left)*, which is why the men in white look much happier than the men in blue. *(Mike Roberts, L.M.P.A.)*

Ed in his sulky at the racetrack, with his great friend Boehm's Eagle
in harness

The "Giant Panda Cub" is a parting gift to my little friends at the Children's Palace in Shanghai, December 1974. They named the porcelain cub Ling-Ling after the real one given by Chairman Mao to the zoo in Washington, D.C.

At the Great Wall of China with our Chinese interpreter-guide.
Frank and Maurice are wearing warm Chinese headgear; my fluffy
white mink hat and coat caused great excitement.

Sheik Mohammed Ashwami, another "instant Boehm collector," especially loved the "Peregrine Falcon" and said it looked as though it might take off.

In the studio with the famous birds of peace, the "Mute Swans"

Ed and I with his porcelain sculpture of the "Ivory-Billed Wood-peckers," an endangered species. Getting Ed to pose for a formal portrait was not easy.

19

Ed Boehm, My Genius Husband

Everyone who met Ed Boehm remembers having met him. He was obviously cut from a special mold. He was striking-looking but, more often than not, dressed in a totally informal manner, like a workman, regardless of the occasion. If anyone around him was discussing a subject that interested him, he would participate with a passionate energy that was almost overwhelming. If it was a subject that did not interest him, he would always find an excuse to step away, like having to finish a drawing or tend to a sick bird.

He fascinated me and often aggravated me, too. There was no changing him, so I learned to deal with the aggravation by concentrating on the fascination. Perhaps in today's world of quick divorce and lack of commitment, Ed Boehm and I never would have made it as a married couple. Having grown up in a strict Catholic family, when I married I knew there would be no divorce, so I knew we had to make it work. If I couldn't mold Ed into a proper "gentleman," I would concentrate on his genius and kindness. He, on the other hand, used to chafe at my constant bubbling conversation, my succession of people coming in and out of the house, and my love of going to and giving parties. We often reminded each other that opposites truly

95

attract. I loved and admired him, and he not only loved me but knew I was a necessity in his life, both in organizing his home and in selling his art and making it possible for him to do what he wanted to do most in life—be close to nature.

He was a born winner who didn't like to lose, which is why he was so competitive and determined to win at whatever he chose to do. "Show me a smiling loser," he said, "and I'll show you an idiot." As a result, there was never a moment of leisure in his day. He either was engrossed in a drawing or a sculpture, caring for his creatures, or preparing for a dog, horse, or bird show. When he sculpted one of his first works of art, a boxer dog, he was infinitely happy. He loved art, but he also loved his dogs, and to engage in an activity that combined them both put him into a state of euphoria. He seemed to breathe life into every animal he sculpted, and not until that illusion had been achieved would he consider the piece finished.

Entertaining and being entertained constrained him. Even eating seemed a waste of time in his later years. He often ate straight from the refrigerator, ignoring a lovely meal someone had prepared. Once, when we were the guests of President and Mrs. Lyndon B. Johnson at a White House luncheon, he gave me a little kick under the table in the middle of dessert and whispered, "Let's go."

"Ed, we can't go!" I whispered, hoping no one would hear us. "The president and the First Lady are the first to leave this room. No one leaves ahead of *them.*"

"But Helen," he pleaded, looking as though he had just lost a dear relative, "my horse is racing!" For him, this was a sincere and justifiable reason for walking out on the president of the United States. It would not have surprised me if he had pushed back his chair, approached the president and said, "Sorry, Mr. President. Hope you don't mind, but my horse is running and I must be at the track on time for his race."

Ed would wander into our living room during a big cocktail party, dressed in khakis "fragrant" from spending hours at the farm. Experience taught me over the years not to try to change him or to criticize him for being a nonconformist. He'd just say something like, "Look, if you make me get dressed up like a monkey and go to things like operas, then in reprisal I'll make you go to every single football and baseball game on the eastern seaboard." Opposites attract.

We were two fierce independents long before the women's movement called upon women to lead their own lives and learn to take care of themselves. Ed taught me that the differences between us would help make me as independent and as self-sufficient as he. This was perhaps the most valuable of all the lessons he taught me. We knew our marriage was far more interesting than if we matched one hundred percent. If we flared up against each other every now and then—well, our lives were far spicier because of it. We knew something I wish more young couples realized in today's world: that two people don't have to agree on everything in order to be able to love each other.

We were life partners, business partners, and best friends during the twenty-five years we shared together. We may not have been "a typical American couple," but we certainly made a remarkable combination. Everything we worked hard for seemed touched with success, even though in the beginning the roads to financial success and recognition were long and rough.

Ed was a stubborn man who fought to the end in a dispute when he considered himself in the right. I remember one evening in our New Jersey home when he was entertaining Bill Conway, the distinguished director of the New York Zoological Society, and Dr. Jean Delacour of France, a world authority on birds, especially pheasants. I was preparing dinner in the kitchen when I heard what might be described as a "conversational brawl" going on in the living room. Ed was arguing that the hummingbird's intelligence is superior to that of other birds. I put the dinner on hold. Two hours later the discussion was still not resolved, so I interrupted with the dictum that dinner was now or never. I was unable to change the topic of discussion even during our dinner.

On rare occasions, Ed would be seized by an overwhelming urge to cook. I knew the results would be either delectable or disastrous, never anything in-between. He'd send out one or two staff members to do the marketing (because he didn't know how to do it, and Ed did not like to launch into projects he had not mastered); then he would invite a few guests to share our meal. I never knew who or what to expect at those dinners. He could make an excellent gumbo, sweet potato pie, and corn bread. He thought nothing of spending three hours in the kitchen preparing these dishes for the people he loved.

One night his famous gumbo did not taste as it should. I looked around the table and saw everyone having difficulty swallowing. No one mentioned the gumbo, but everyone began taking giant helpings of the corn bread and sweet potato pie. Ed remained silent, too, and did not press people to take more of his gumbo. He knew what was wrong, but he would not admit it to his guests. He had inadvertently ground up a rubber spatula in the electric "gourmet center," and that had then been cooked in the gumbo.

Ed also loved pop music. He had a deep, clear baritone, but unfortunately he could not carry a tune. So, instead of singing himself, he would ask me to sing for him while he assumed the role of singing coach. He gave endless directions on how to walk, stand, hold my hands, and project my voice. It may not have helped my singing voice, but it certainly helped my presence in public speaking engagements.

When we purchased a farm in Harbourton, New Jersey, just about three miles from our house, Ed initiated the projects that brought him the greatest happiness. He spent the next five years breeding and building one of the country's finest Holstein herds. He raced and bred standardbred horses and bred and showed Holsteins, Angus, and Jerseys. Sometimes for Christmas I would receive not furs or diamonds, but cows.

On our first Christmas Eve after we had purchased the farm, we planned to exchange presents in front of the fireplace after dinner. It was a beautiful snowy night. Ed announced with a measured sadness, "Helen, I forgot your Christmas gift. Stupid of me! I left it on my desk in the farm office."

I told him that was perfectly all right. I would finish cleaning up while he drove over to fetch it.

"Come along with me, Helen," he pleaded. "It's so beautiful outside. The snow is falling, and the farm will look like a Christmas card painting."

We drove three miles in the snowstorm, and by the time we walked into Ed's office, I was really excited about what treasure awaited me. But there was nothing on his desk.

"I must have left it in the barn," he said, "Come on in here."

We went into the barn toward the rear and finally came to the calving section. There on the hay lay four newborn Jersey calves. They looked at me with enormous velvety brown eyes. Each wore a thin chain with a gold locket resting in the middle of its forehead. The lockets were engraved with "H. F. Boehm."

"Oh, Ed!" I said, putting my arms around him, "just what I wanted. Four calves."

When we returned home I gave Ed his present, a French malachite and bronze doré clock from Aspreys in London. He grinned, put his arms around me, and said, "Oh, Helen, just what *you* wanted!"

If Ed wanted a particular cow or horse badly enough and there was no imminent birthday or anniversary to celebrate, he'd try to sneak it onto the farm and pretend it had been there all along. Now and then I would try the same thing with a designer dress or a fur. If Ed asked me about it, I would reply, "What, this old thing? You've seen it before! Don't you remember when I wore it last Easter?"

Ed would nod his head and say, "Oh yes, sure I remember," convinced that it was indeed something that he had forgotten by being merely unobservant.

Ed christened our farm with a rather aristocratic-sounding, Scottish kind of name, "Duncravin." At first he wouldn't tell me the significance of the name, simply explaining that he liked the sound of it. That was enough reason. Finally he decided to tell me. When he was about to return home to Maryland after service in the air force in 1944 and a fire completely destroyed his farm and cattle, he began dreaming of owning a farm again. Now that this dream was finally realized, he was "done craving."

Although Ed only went to church twice during our marriage (once was for our wedding), he was a man of deep religious feelings. Often, on my way to Sunday mass, I would try to persuade him to join me. He was always busy with a mare to foal, a cow to calf, a sculpture to finish, a dog to whelp, an important letter to write, or a bird to nurture. One snowy Sunday, as I was leaving for mass, he took me to the dining room window and pointed outside to a magnificent male cardinal, a flash of scarlet on our evergreen tree branch.

"Look, Helen. That's God's work, too. I hear the Lord's sermon in nature every single day." I could not quarrel with that. He probably thought about God many more times a day than the "Sunday knee-benders," as we often call ourselves.

Ed was no Lothario who spouted beautiful words of love; but he always made me feel loved. Every once in a while he would remind me that we were partners in more ways than one. One time he looked at his aviaries and suddenly put his arms around me. "Helen, I don't tell you this in words all the time, but I hope you realize that I *know* none of this would be here in my life without you. I lead the kind of life I love today because of you."

I am reminded many times every day that if Ed Boehm had not come along, none of the life I lead and love today would have been possible either.

I'm glad people still think of us together, as a team, when they talk about either of us. Once I was complaining to a friend and confidante about Ed's manners at social functions. "Listen, Helen," she said sharply, "don't you ever complain about that. For one thing, you're married to a terrific guy, and he's *all man.*"

As I look around me today, her wisdom is even sharper. Ed Boehm was certainly all man.

20

Acquisitions Are the Sure Sign of Success

I had always craved beautiful things, and it was a long time before I was able to buy them. My life with Ed had been happy, but we were usually flat broke while trying to get the Boehm operation launched properly with a healthy cash flow. I had gone without during the first twelve years of our married life and had grown weary of calling on stores via Greyhound bus. Whenever I took the train to and from cities, I left at six o'clock in the morning and returned at midnight in order not to have to pay for an overnight hotel room.

For the first twelve years I had neither jewels nor furs, but I always considered them important simply because others judge your success at first glance by how you are dressed. Though I disliked it intensely, I originally used the trade entrances in stores like Tiffany's because of having to carry so many great big boxes with me. I had the feeling that the store executives would want me to use the trade entrance anyway, with or without boxes. But when I appeared in my first new fur coat, a tourmaline mink coat of a soft peach color, I felt extremely royal. It was an instant metamorphosis. I found that as soon as I wore it into the great jewelry stores of America, I was able to deal directly with the top management instead of someone down the line. (This was a good rationalization for what has become a lifelong support of the fur industry!)

I first started wearing jewelry when I lectured at the Dallas Women's Club. This formidable group of women, attired in the latest designer dresses and wearing their incredible jewels at noon, were the inspiration for my going to my good friends and business associates at Caldwell Jewelers to borrow a twenty-karat cat's eye ring. As I stood in the receiving line wearing my brown broadtail skirt and jacket with jeweled buttons, I saw the women scrutinizing my attire with admiration. In my mind there was only one brown broadtail suit in the world—mine. Then they saw my twenty-karat cat's eye ring and several pairs of Texan eyes opened wide in astonishment. I decided this was the way for me to go. If I dressed with such opulence, the public would react that Boehm must be doing pretty well.

As we made more money, and as Ed added more birds to the aviary and gardens to our place, my jewelry box became more laden, too. Ed loved to see me wearing fine things, not because of their value but because of their intrinsic beauty. Years before, he had even helped me cut out the patterns for the dresses I sewed for special sales trips. Now we could buy a ruby and diamond necklace, and then a few years later, a bracelet to match. I realized I could now give presents to myself, something I had never done before. I first purchased a large ruby ring to add to my collection, bought at auction at Asprey's in London.

Jewels were not the only thing on my mind as we became more successful. Ever since the Franzolin kids first piled into the family automobile for Sunday outings, I have loved cars. I like them big and showy, most particularly beautiful vintage cars. Ed, however, did not share my automobile enthusiasms. He looked upon any car like a farmer looks upon a truck, as something necessary for hauling purposes.

One of the distinguished collectors attending the first Boehm exhibition at Asprey's in London was a Mr. Barclay, who with his lovely wife had just purchased a pair of Boehm birds. When Mr. Asprey introduced the head of the Rolls Royce Company to me at the reception, Mr. Barclay asked, "How long will you be staying in London, Mrs. Boehm?" I noticed he carried a beautiful hand-carved walking stick.

"Another ten days or so," I answered, thinking how exciting it was to meet the man for whose ancestors the famous Barclay Square in London had been named.

"Where are you staying?" he asked.

"At Claridge's."

"Well, Mrs. Boehm, I would like to provide you with a car while you're in England." He didn't specify what type of car or what color, and I did not know what his intention was. But this was an offer I couldn't refuse.

The following morning, the concierge rang and announced in a very grand tone, "Madam, your car is waiting."

When I walked down the hotel steps I could hardly believe the glistening apparition in front of me. There was the most beautiful car I had ever seen: a brand new white Rolls Royce, complete with a tall English chauffeur appropriately attired in uniform, complete with boots and gloves. The car had that delicious new smell and everything inside and out had been lovingly hand-polished. The burled elm dashboard was jeweler magnificent. It was 1964, and that was probably the first white Rolls to appear in Mayfair.

I sank back into the seat. This was certainly a fantasy; the atmosphere was too luxurious to be real.

"What is your pleasure, madam?" The velvet tones of the driver matched the Rolls' interior.

"Harrod's please."

To continue the fantasy of the day, I went into Harrod's and purchased some beautiful plump white grapes from Belgium that cost $8 a pound. I saved every seed because I wanted to grow my own white grapes in New Jersey. (I am still waiting for that vineyard to sprout.)

The following day, the concierge again called to announce that my "car and driver were waiting." This time I took along two friends and we went shopping on Bond Street and then to tea at the Savoy. I decided even the tea tasted better because of the Rolls.

When I returned from my outing, there was a call from Mr. Barclay: "Mrs. Boehm, why don't you take the car home with you to America? It's quite obvious you love it. You should have it. You quite deserve it."

That was the catch phrase—I *deserved* it.

It was terribly tempting, but what would Ed say?

"Mr. Barclay," I heard myself saying, "I'd love to, but I just can't. I'm going back on the ship and it wouldn't work out. Besides, my husband would not be very pleased if I did."

I decided to add a bit of humor. "The only way I could take it back is if it had an American eagle on the bonnet!" I knew that such a silly remark would go unheeded, since it would be unthinkable to remove the famous "flying lady."

Mr. Barclay was undaunted. The following day the car and driver pulled up in front of Claridge's again. Mr. Barclay had removed the flying lady from the bonnet of the white Rolls and had replaced it with a shining American eagle! The car door even had my monogram in place. I couldn't *not* take it now. I must take the eagle back home where it belonged. But, my God, how would I ever pay for it? How would I sneak it into the garage so Ed wouldn't see it? How would I ever explain it to Ed?

Fortune smiled on me. (Fortune always has.) Coming over to England on board the S.S. *France,* I had met an executive with Morgan Guaranty Bank. He had just been appointed director of the London branch, and he had repeated several times that I should call upon him if I ever needed anything. I certainly needed him now. One telephone call and, without fuss or delay, he arranged for a check to be sent immediately to Mr. Barclay. I have banked at Morgan ever since.

And so the car and I went home on the S.S. *France.* As it was driven on board, I watched it anxiously. It seemed that hundreds of people were watching it, too, making a big fuss over it. I heard shouts of *"mais, c'est formidable!" "C'est un bâteau blanc!"* ("It's a white ship!")

About ten miles offshore, I made a ship-to-shore call. The line was poor, and I could hardly hear Frank Cosentino's voice on the other end.

"Frank, Frank, are you there?"

"Yes, Mrs. Boehm. You needn't shout, I hear you. Where are you?"

"I'm about ten miles outside New York harbor. And Frank, guess what? You'll be so pleased—I won a white Rolls Royce in a raffle!"

"Mrs. Boehm, you'll have to do better than that. Mr. Boehm will *never* fall for that."

"Okay, but, Frank, please meet me and drive it home. It's easy to handle because the steering wheel is on the left side like ours, and it has power steering. I'm much too nervous about Ed's reaction to drive it myself. And, please, whatever you do, don't tell Ed about it."

I loved that car. I felt such elation as we drove from New York back to Washington Crossing. The car was an object of total luxury, but as we neared the house, I began to worry about Ed's reaction. The fear became exaggerated as we drove up the long driveway to the house. The car glided to a smooth stop, and I rushed right into Ed's arms, hoping to distract him with hugs and cries of hello. The car was hardly inconspicuous, however; it loomed behind me, as Frank later commented, "like a tall-masted schooner in full sail."

"What's that, Helen?" Ed asked disbelievingly, looking in the direction of the Rolls. He blinked his eyes as if to make sure he was seeing what he saw.

"What's what?" I innocently replied, looking over his shoulder in still another direction.

The Rolls was the cause of a great many arguments. At one point Ed actually chipped a bit of paint from it, muttering, "Look at that terrible workmanship!"

When the car rolled into our swimming pool one day, I think Ed Boehm was actually delighted. Ed had left early that morning for his studio. When I went out to get into the car, I realized I was not dressed warmly enough, so I left the engine running and dashed back into the house to change. A few seconds later there was a terrible, crashing sound outside, as though the house had exploded.

The housekeeper and I rushed to the window and looked out upon a surrealist nightmare. There was my lovely white Rolls, half sunken, half floating in the swimming pool. With a marked note of hysteria in my voice, I telephoned Ed for help. His maddening reaction as he arrived at the house to survey the scene was laughter, not sympathy.

In reflection, I think Ed Boehm must have psyched that car right into the swimming pool.

It required six men working with a derrick for two and a half hours to extricate the car from the pool. The scene was reminiscent of a bad gangster film. Several weeks later, after a very complicated and expensive restoration, the car was ready for me to use again.

One day, I had to leave early by train for New York. I felt it inappropriate to drive myself to the local station in a white Rolls and leave it parked there, so I took Ed's car. I left him a note at 6:30 in the morning: "Dear Ed, I'm taking your Lincoln today to leave at the station, so do use my Rolls."

The next day I was once again behind the wheel of my car to drive to our office in Trenton, when I was struck by a foul odor. I assumed that Ed must have driven the car to the farm, wearing his dirty boots. I quickly opened the windows on both sides to let in some air, and a cloud of feathers began to swirl about in the car. I turned around, and there on the thick beige lambs' wool carpeting was a covering of feathers, food, and even droppings. Ed had transported his fancy fowl to a show in the back seat of my precious Rolls Royce!

This incident taught me one great lesson. Never again would I borrow Ed's car, because who knew what he would do next to my Rolls.

21

England Takes on a Special Meaning

The British Isles were to become an area of great importance to our company in the fairly early days of our growth. By 1963 I knew we were successful enough to tackle Europe. At first Ed did not favor this idea. To him it was just another of my "unnecessary" business promotions. But since Ed never wrote a check in his life and I was the one who met the payroll and managed the expenses, I managed to convince him that this was a sound idea. We would have to go to England first, the country from which every American bride dreamed of ordering her dinnerware.

My first job would be to find one store in London that would agree to serve as the official representative for Boehm porcelain throughout the United Kingdom. This presented a bona fide dilemma. My two favorite stores were Thomas Goode and Asprey & Co. It was impossible to choose, because both were superior establishments. The solution may have been daring and undoable, but I managed it by offering representation to *both* Asprey and Goode, provided they would jointly sponsor an opening exhibition of Boehm porcelain. That was like asking Bulgari and Van Cleef to do a joint showing of their jewels.

Much to everyone's surprise, especially Ed's, the archrivals agreed. The exhibition was scheduled for June 1964 at the London Hilton Hotel.

Ed knew he must create a very special, "knock 'em dead" piece for the English show. It was the type of challenge he and his artisans adored. After mulling it over for several days, he came up with the idea of a large piece representing male and female ivory-billed woodpeckers with their young. The piece, when fired, stood five feet tall and weighed one hundred pounds. It was one of the largest and certainly one of the most complex works ever undertaken by the Boehm studio.

The casting of the wings began on a Friday evening; it took until Sunday night before a perfect set was completed. Ed and several of his assistants slept on cots in the studio, catching only a few hours of sleep. The pressure to finish in time was agonizing. The key problem, of course, was with the individual clay feathers. Some were seven inches long and so thin they kept falling off. The men kept at it, drinking numerous cups of coffee and occasionally running around the block to get some air and relieve the tension. The end result was triumphant. We priced the "Woodpecker" at $20,000. Ed said that "absolutely no one will ever buy such costly porcelain in England, especially by an unknown maker." In my mind, there was never any doubt. I was confident, as always, that someone would fall in love with it. Someone did. The "Woodpecker" was the first piece sold.

I sailed for England on the S.S. *France* and naturally took advantage of the captive shipboard audience to polish my selling technique. As one of my friends on the trip wrote to me later, "If there were only two people in a room, in five minutes you would talk at least one of them into buying a Boehm porcelain. In ten minutes, you would have found two buyers!"

Ed made special exhibition tables for me to use on the S.S. *France*. The birds were embedded at least one inch deep into wooden shelves especially made for the exhibit, thus protecting them from a rocky voyage. In those days, I did all the packing and unpacking of the birds, and I became a display director of sorts through necessity. On that trip, I managed by myself to hold a porcelain show, exhibit various Boehm pieces, and run films on how porcelain is made. There was no one in First Class who debarked from that ship who had not been "Boehm-ized" during the trip. I have never been one to ignore a floating target of opportunity!

I found another target of opportunity in London. I dropped by the U.S. Embassy to inform them about the Boehm exhibition to be jointly sponsored by Asprey's and Goode's. I used the occasion to suggest to embassy officials that an American eagle, like the one that had been presented to President John F. Kennedy in 1961, should be exhibited at the embassy in London to commemorate the late president. Ambassador David Bruce thought it was a splendid idea and accepted the sculpture on September 14, 1964, on behalf of the embassy, where it is now on permanent exhibition.

22

The *S.S. France* Docks along the Delaware River

Without a doubt, my favorite ship was always the *S.S. France.* I crossed the Atlantic on her at least a dozen times, collecting many friends and Boehm supporters along the way. One of my favorite cruise friends, Don Atkins, director of the Morgan Guaranty Bank in Barclay Square, London, helped me purchase my famous white Rolls Royce.

The crew of the ship makes or breaks any long voyage, and the captain is as important as the engine, as far as I'm concerned. I had many reasons to say thank you to Captain Ropars and Purser Roger Joubert (who often sat me at the captain's table and did so many favors for me), so I decided to give them a party.

I made it a black-tie dinner dance at our Washington Crossing home. Our guests of honor wore their dress naval uniforms. The American garden was converted into a Parisian street café. The menu was French. I had the waiters and waitresses dressed like Moulin Rouge dancers, and the place cards and menu cards came from the *France.* The musicians were dressed in French costumes, too, and played the current popular music from France. The centerpiece on each table was a model of the liner afloat on a sea of blue bachelor buttons, representing the

110

Atlantic. I decorated the ten tables for six with white cloths, crisscrossed with wide satin ribbons in blue, white, and red to further reinforce the French theme. The guest list was comprised of sixty friends I had met aboard the liner on various trips. The dinner was an occasion that marked many sentimental reunions.

Everyone had a marvelous time except Ed. If our guests had been a group of wildlife game wardens or horse auctioneers, he would have been interested in attending the dinner, but the First Class passengers of the *S.S. France* held an extremely low priority in his life. Getting Ed into a black tie was almost impossible, and a French party with all the trimmings was much too "Hollywood" for him. Furthermore, he was incensed that this party was taking place adjacent to his African aviaries, the home of his rare imported birds. These birds were accustomed to the stillness of a dark night, and Ed was convinced our party was going to throw them all into whatever kind of hysteria birds can suffer from. I had a feeling that if anything did indeed happen to them this night, my head would go on the block.

I made four trips from the garden to the house to fetch Ed, all to no avail. He was lying comfortably on the bed, watching the World Series. The game was an exciting one, and once when I remonstrated with him and urged him to "come join our guests," he looked at me in disbelief. "Helen!" he cried. "The bases are loaded. You expect me to leave this game *now*? At this point?"

When the main course was ready to be served, the master of the house finally appeared, dressed as if he were going walking with the dogs, in beige slacks, a knit polo shirt, and a tweed jacket. I said nothing, thinking homicide the only action merited at this point, but at least he had appeared. He went around the tables, greeting everyone, and then sat down. I could tell he was already longing to leave this glittering scene and return to the "real world" of baseball games, birds, and horses. It was impossible not to remember the remark he'd made when he proposed to me: "I'll always be a headache, but I'll never be a bore." Ed Boehm was a man of his word.

When the waiter brought him the main course, I knew he was not going to eat it. He asked the waiter to summon Haralene, our housekeeper, from the kitchen. He whispered that he wanted a sandwich of "Genoa salami with lettuce and tomatoes," which she immediately produced and personally brought to the table. I looked around my table at my guests, gave a Gallic shrug, and came out with one of the few French expressions I know, "*C'est la vie.*"

The party broke up just past midnight. Lang, my chauffeur at that time, had finished his dinner in the breakfast room and sat waiting to drive Captain Ropars and Monsieur Joubert back to the *France,* which was berthed at Pier 46 in Manhattan. I bid them goodnight after presenting each with a five-foot-tall plush chimpanzee for their daughters. It was a joyful way to say goodnight and bid them a safe journey back to France. We all watched them settle sleepily into the back of the white Rolls Royce.

Lang returned at 4 A.M. and reported that he had encountered many strange stares as he stopped for lights in New York. Passersby who looked into the interior must have wondered a little at the sight of two distinguished, elegantly uniformed men, fast alseep, their chins resting on the heads of two enormous stuffed chimpanzees.

What mattered to me was the fact that two young girls in France were going to be very happy when their fathers returned home.

23

The Cruelest Moment
of Them All

Death be not proud, though some have
called thee Mighty and dreadful, for thou
art not so.

—John Donne

By the late 1960s I had become used to being on the road for Boehm porcelains five months out of the year. Ed had become used to it, too. We survived only because of our nightly telephone check-ins. Those were *long* conversations, sometimes of an hour's duration. I never saw the telephone bills, but they must have been monumental. When I was away, I knew that Frank Cosentino was at the helm, managing the business aspects, and that Ed was spending hours planning, doing research, sketching, and laying out the artistic direction of the company for two-, five-, and ten-year periods. Our housekeeper made nutritious meals for Ed, but she complained to no avail that he never came to the table on time. Without his wife around to chide him into coming to dinner, he remained sculpting, drawing, and studying his beloved animals, birds, and flowers until well after dinnertime.

113

Finally he would come to the table, totally unaware that the food, which by now had been reheated several times, was not as good as it would have been two hours earlier.

My trips were essential to the business. I spent my time courting store owners and department managers, thinking up ideas for attracting publicity, giving lectures to important women's groups, and, the most important activity of all, talking to the customers who came into the Boehm section of the store. I learned to read each customer, to understand his or her life-style, to be sensitive to the spark that ignited in the mind of a young collector. With each one I learned a lesson in selling and in "closing the deal." Each customer also learned a lot from me, too. I talked about Ed's life as an animal lover, about his humble beginnings as an artist, about his experimentations with the medium of hard-paste porcelain. I never did it just to close a sale. It was inside me, always ready to emerge with force. My enthusiasm for the work of the Boehm studio was boundless.

Ed once asked me if it wasn't wasting time to talk at length to someone who obviously looked as though he or she did not have the means to buy anything, much less a thousand dollar porcelain. I replied, "Ed, leave the selling to me. Half the people who look as though they don't have a dime in their pockets are very rich; and the other half know people who are rich and can help bring them in to buy."

The on-the-road life took a lot out of me. The hardest part was being away from Ed. We talked about this often and agreed that it had to be. I was an essential ingredient in the success of the company. We were partners in the true sense of the word, and I had to play my role.

In January of 1969 I finished an especially arduous tour of the Southwest that culminated in a special ceremony at the Santa Fe Museum, where a collection of Boehm porcelains was formally presented. With Ed's approval, I flew to Dallas to spend three days at the Greenhouse, a wonderful spa in which to rest, lose weight, unwind, and become a human being once again. Ed insisted I go there once a year, and on this trip, I needed it more than I ever had in my entire life.

Ed sounded fine on the telephone my first night there. I told him all about the Museum of New Mexico at Santa Fe and the delight of the guests when they first saw the porcelain "Roadrunner," their state bird. I described the entrance to the museum, charmingly lit with brown paper bags partially filled with sand and holding lighted candles. I told him about the wonderful Mexican food at dinner and how surprised I was when they presented me with a twenty-pound solid silver brick as a remembrance of my trip to Santa Fe. We laughed over our different ideas on what to do with the silver brick.

The next afternoon Frank Cosentino called me.

"Mrs. Boehm," he said with almost a cheerful voice, because I could tell he did not want to worry me too much, "Mr. Boehm had slight chest pains this morning. The doctor felt that as a precaution we should put him in the hospital for twenty-four hours of observation."

"My God, Frank, is it serious?" I felt my own heart rapidly increasing its rate of speed.

"It is probably not serious at all. They just want to make a lot of tests."

"How did he get to the hospital?"

"The doctor's secretary drove him in her own car." I felt relieved. He had not even gone in an ambulance.

Frank laughed. "You can imagine what it was like, not only getting him to the hospital but admitting him. It was like harnessing a wild horse. That husband of yours is tough!"

"He sounded fine on the telephone last night, Frank."

"He *was* fine. I talked to him for over an hour myself. He had been watching the Knicks on television [a New York professional basketball team]. He went over every point with me, refereeing the play from the sidelines."

"I'll call him right now," I said, feeling a wonderful wave of relief. Nothing had really happened to Ed. He was going to be fine. I knew it. He was in his mid-fifties. You can't keep a tough hombre like Ed Boehm down with an illness. He had never been sick. He was going to be fine.

"Don't call him, Mrs. Boehm," Frank said, still without gravity in his voice. "The doctor has ordered absolute quiet while these tests are going on."

It seemed very odd that I could not call Ed. It was the first time in our twenty-five years of married life that I could not call him. After changing my reservations so I could leave for Newark on the first flight out of Dallas in the morning, I began to pack.

Our plane landed at 10:30 the next morning. The minute I came through the gangway into the airport, I froze. I was expecting our driver, Lang, to meet me. Instead, I saw Frank, Lang, a nurse in a white uniform, and a wheelchair.

It hit me right away.

Frank put his arms around me and said, "Mr. Boehm died in his sleep early this morning of a massive heart attack. Come on, we're going to get out of here and go home."

The nurse gave me a sedative, somehow we made it home, and somehow we arranged a beautiful funeral service worthy of Ed. I had him dressed in his best "Ed clothes"—not the traditional dark suit and white shirt, but in a new suede jacket I had bought him in Houston, dark brown slacks, a beige shirt, and a tie with birds on it.

I don't think I would have made it through those days without Frank. He was Ed's best friend, our closest colleague, and really a member of our family. He knew what to do and shouldered the load of organizing the funeral and seeing to the legal aspects of what was for me the most terrible time of my life. I remembered all the pain and anguish of my mother's and father's deaths, and I listened closely once again to the priest's assurance that we would "all meet again" one day in the next life. I believed in that thoroughly.

The world must go on, but I dreaded what lay ahead. A week after Ed's death, four grieving people sat around the teak conference table in our building on Trenton's Fairfacts Street, pondering the future of a company whose entire existence had depended upon the work of a person who was now dead. I finally sat up straight in my chair and said, "Enough of this!" This company was to continue.

I made myself chairman of the company and asked Frank Cosentino to assume the presidency. We would look forward. Harold Coleman, our attorney, and Frank Suplee, our accountant, helped cheer us by making remarks such as "Ed has trained those artisans in the studio to *perfection*. They can and they *should* continue their work, but they need to be led." Harold remarked, "Helen, you have always been out in front in the marketplace. You know what the buyers and their customers want. You can decide what should be made." Then he said something that made me stop short. "Helen," he said, "you've always told Ed what to make anyway, ever since he really got going in this business."

It was true. When the business became successful, it was I who informed Ed of the changes of taste in the marketplace. It was I who led him away from his large animals into the more delicate birds and the flowers. It was I who had spotted "targets of opportunity," like making "The Polo Player" as a gift for Queen Elizabeth.

I looked around the table. "Gentlemen," I said, "we will go on. This company will grow and prosper." I looked over at Frank. "All we need," I said, looking up at the ceiling as though I hoped God were listening hard, "is a sign that we will be accepted even though Ed Boehm is dead."

The sign came. Call it a miracle, good luck, or coincidence— call it what you will. Not too long after, by making the most difficult piece we'd ever undertaken—the large mute swans, the "Birds of Peace"—we would prove to collectors, buyers, and consumers that we were still in business—and how! At Ed's death, the collectors had felt it would be the end of the company. Store buyers had called up anxiously, inquiring about future shipments and making plans to buy from other art sources to fill their shelves. Everyone, except for the people gathered in the conference room on Fairfacts Street that day, felt that Boehm Porcelain had come to an end.

They didn't know the Franzolin family. We're made of tough fiber.

24

A Presidential Assist

When Richard Nixon was vice-president, he knew and admired Ed's work. In 1968, shortly before his winning the presidential election, I caught a glimpse of him at a special showing of the late President Eisenhower's paintings and memorabilia.

"Helen Boehm," he said with a mischievous grin, "when we get to the White House, we'll start ordering those state gifts from your talented husband."

Eight days after Richard Nixon was sworn into office, Ed Boehm died. The president kept his word and used Boehm porcelains throughout his term of office. When he wrote me in early February 1969 that he would like to use Boehm porcelains as his official gifts to all the heads of state he would be visiting on his forthcoming NATO tour, it meant that Boehm birds would be given to Harold Wilson, Heinrich Luebke, Mariano Rumor, Maurice Couve de Murville, and His Holiness Pope Paul VI—rather a stellar group.

What a coup! The president's selection of Boehm gave everyone in our studio and in our retail outlets a tremendous boost. It was a sad period in my life, mourning the loss of my husband, but the letter from President Nixon was a strong signal that the business of porcelains would continue to grow.

When Nixon returned from his NATO trip, he wrote me describing the enthusiastic acceptance given the porcelains by the heads of state. It seemed logical to me that it was time to donate a permanent Boehm collection to the White House in memory of my husband. President Nixon replied that this would be a fine idea. The proper exchange of calls and letters was then made, setting up the details of the final arrangements.

When the day of installation came, I dressed in monochromatic grays—a soft designer suit, darker gray shoes and handbag—and, sporting a bird pin on my lapel, drove to 1600 Pennsylvania Avenue with Frank Cosentino and Dominic Angelini, our studio manager. As we began preparing the shelves in the Oval Office for the birds, we noticed they were extremely wobbly. I asked the head usher, J. B. West, if there was any way the shelves could be replaced. J. B. took us to the carpenters' shop in the basement, and in a matter of hours the White House carpenters and Dominic Angelini had constructed new shelves. They were painted and lined with moiré silk. There is no "impossible situation" at the White House. Every problem is solved. I will never forget how those carpenters jumped in within minutes to help us out.

While we were finishing the arranging of the birds on the shelves, J. B. West came to tell me there would be an official dedication of the Boehm porcelains. This was a total surprise; the three of us were excited and delighted beyond description.

It was August 21, 1969, the day Ed would have been fifty-six years old. President Nixon came in with a phalanx of reporters, photographers, and TV network crews. He spoke admiringly about Ed Boehm's work and told me that our carrying on what had by now become a great American art form was very important for our country. One of the reporters asked a question I thought was very pointed: "Are there any hawks or doves in this collection?"

President Nixon laughed. "Of course not. This is a collection of peaceful and beautiful birds. Mrs. Boehm has chosen birds that are the favorites of all Americans."

I suddenly had an idea.

"Mr. President," I interjected, "maybe we should have a new symbol for a 'bird of peace' for the world. After all, the dove is somewhat tarnished as a symbol and not all countries recognize it."

The president replied, "That's a great idea, Mrs. Boehm. You've got the job." I was astonished to hear the reporters applauding this conversation.

The minute we returned to Trenton, the studio began the task of finding the perfect new bird of peace. I wrote to Ed's great friends: Dr. Delacour in France, Sir Edward Halstrom in Australia, and zoo directors in many countries. I asked for their suggestions for a new "bird of peace" to be used for the world. One of the suggestions that came back was a phoenix bird ripping out its feathers from its chest. This was rejected because I wanted a bird to end wars, not begin them! Another suggestion that was quickly (but diplomatically) rejected came from one of the eminent people we referred to—that the bird be named after *him*. Finally we unanimously agreed that the bird would be the mute swan, representing serenity and purity, a bird that had been associated with peace throughout history and in mythology. The mute swan's range is worldwide; it came to the shores of America during the nineteenth century. Perhaps its most important characteristic is that it speaks with a soft voice. Dillon Ripley, the distinguished head of the Smithsonian in Washington and a great bird fancier, concurred that the mute swan should become the new worldwide symbol for peace.

The choice artistically was a difficult one. A smaller bird would have been far easier. A pair of these swans took two years and ten tons of plaster to make. Many artisans were involved. It required four men just to cast one section; sixty thousand feathered barbs had to be detailed on the model. And then we added three young cygnets and lily pads to the ground base. It was a work of art that represented nature and birds in their loveliest, most natural state.

At that time, of course, I had no idea the swans would be going to China. What was important to me was that they were a symbol not only to our collectors but also to our artisans that Boehm porcelain was going ahead. We were able to carry out any difficult challenge, no matter how technically complicated.

I kept the White House informed of the studio's progress on

the swans during those next two years. When the piece was finally finished, a call came from the White House.

"Mrs. Boehm, the president would like to purchase the 'Mute Swans' as his gift to the people of China for our forthcoming trip early in 1972."

I felt the tears trickling out of the corners of my eyes as I told him how much this meant to me, to my company and to everyone who had ever been associated with Boehm. It was the real sign of encouragement we had needed after Ed's death.

Yes, it was a turning point. The "Birds of Peace" made the important and visible statement that the Boehm studio had the talent and know-how to create something that was far beyond what anyone else in the field of porcelain was able to do. I felt stronger, both as a woman and as a businessperson, than I ever had before in my life.

25

Upstaging the President's Publicity

President and Mrs. Nixon often invited me to state dinners and functions. I had been to White House state luncheons in the Eisenhower administration, but it is an honor and always a thrill to go in any administration, particularly to a state dinner.

In 1970 I was invited to an especially important White House reception. I originally planned to make the drive to Washington in my white Rolls Royce with my lifelong American driver and friend Langston Burrell. However, Mr. and Mrs. Shelley Acuff, close friends, insisted on doing "something special" for me and offered me the use of their brand-new Cadillac limousine. Thinking the Acuffs' black car would be more understated and appropriate at a White House entrance, I accepted.

Late that afternoon, just after we had pulled onto the throughway headed for Washington, we had a flat tire. I didn't think much about it because I knew Lang could easily fix it. (He had been with General Motors for twenty-five years and knew everything there was to know about cars.) But I didn't count on what Lang discovered when he opened the trunk: There was no jack.

Lang, a handsome six-foot-four black man, stood beside the car, gesturing for other cars to stop. A number of people slowed down, stopped, and then drove on. This happened over and over again, so finally I rolled down the window and shouted to Lang, "Why don't they want to help us, Lang?"

"Mrs. Boehm, I didn't want to worry you, but there's a special type jack for this new model, and none of them have it."

"Never mind, Lang, I'll come stand with you and with my white handkerchief we'll flag down a truck."

After about half an hour, a great big red trailer truck with two men in it pulled over. (By this time I was getting nervous about being on time for the White House reception.) A large, burly driver came over to us. I smiled, "Hello, fellows. I'm in trouble. I'm due at the White House in less than two hours, and we still have an hour and a half to go. Can you please help us out?"

"Yeah, yeah, lady. The White House. That's what they all say."

"It's true, I'll show you my invitation! How about fifty dollars?" (In those days, that was a handsome offer.)

Looking pleased, the truck driver said, "Lady, for that price I'll do it with my teeth!"

In less than fifteen minutes, we were back on the road, zooming toward 1600 Pennsylvania Avenue. I had run my stockings and had grabbed a pair of pantyhose on my way to the car. In order to save time, I decided to put them on in the back seat and asked Lang to turn the rear-view mirror away. We were fighting against time.

When we reached Washington, I immediately went to the Madison Hotel, where I was preregistered. I started to get into my beautiful new Stavropoulos, a draped gown in creamy white chiffon. But I was so nervous about doing up all the buttons and the long zipper myself that I called Garfinckel's, a famous Washington store nearby that also carried Boehm porcelain. After explaining my plight to the couture salon, they promised to send over a dresser immediately.

I had barely hung up when there was a knock on the door to my suite. A man stood outside and greeted me affably with, "May I help you, Mrs. Boehm? I'm your dresser."

I was a little shocked to discover my dresser was a male, but I thought, Oh, well, there's no time to be prissy about this. He did the job beautifully and with utmost tact and speed. Within minutes I was ready to go.

As I tried to open the door to the hallway, the lock jammed. The dresser and I pulled and pushed, but it wouldn't budge. "I don't believe this," I said to myself, and then out loud into the phone to the front desk. Up came two engineers with screw-drivers, 3-in-1 Oil, and an enormous bag of tools. It took another fifteen minutes of precious time, but they got me out.

I was the very last guest to arrive at the White House, but I made it—just as the sound of "Hail to the Chief" announced the arrival of President and Mrs. Nixon. I was quite out of breath, all the more so in the excitement of discovering that my escort for the evening was Billy Graham. His blue eyes were shining in his tanned and handsome face as he gallantly took my hand under his arm, patted it reassuringly, and said, "You're right on time, Mrs. Boehm. And you look beautiful." His gracious manner and warmth had a soothing effect on me, and in the moment or two it took to reach the receiving line, I forgot all my misadventures.

The beauty of the scene that night during the state dinner was unforgettable. The men looked handsome in their white tie and tails, the women glamorous in their floating dresses with jewels that sparkled beneath the crystal chandeliers. The U-shaped table was splendidly decked with silver-gilt candelabra and tall urns filled with flowers. It was like a still life painting; so was the dinner itself, sliced roast pheasant served from platters centered by stuffed pheasant in full plumage. My dinner partner, Billy Graham, was a wonderful conversationalist, so much so that I very naughtily ignored the government official on my other side, and I caught looks of hostility from the woman on Billy's other side, too.

I woke up in the hotel later thinking the entire glittering evening had been a dream. Ed would have been proud to see me at that dinner, even though he would have refused to don white tie and tails for anyone. The next morning I absentmindedly picked up the copy of the *Washington Post* that was tucked up alongside the orange juice and croissants on my breakfast tray, and there was the story of the state dinner in black and white. The picture of President and Mrs. Nixon headlined the story and various guests were accorded a respectable paragraph—that is, until it came to "Mrs. Edward Marshall Boehm." A member of the press had overheard my description of my misadventures and recorded the story almost word for word, from changing the tire to being locked in my hotel suite with a dresser. I had quite innocently upstaged the president and his guest of state.

26

The Wildlife Princes

It was important to me to be able to continue Ed's commitment to wildlife preservation, since our livelihood depended on nature, and after his death I threw myself into wildlife preservation work with enough energy for both of us. Through my association with two organizations in particular, I came to feel almost like a postdoctoral student in the field.

"The handsome prince who always wore a white carnation"—this was the founder and moving force of the 1001 Nature Trust, Prince Bernhard of the Netherlands, who successfully led the Trust through its beginning days early in the 1960s. Forty countries were involved in the group's effort to preserve endangered species of flora and fauna, and each private member showed his commitment by paying many thousands of dollars to belong (as did I). As its president, the prince used his considerable charm to raise money for his favorite charity, and indeed stopped at little to do so.

I remember what a charming way he had of finding out—especially if, as in my case, you were a widow or widower—whether you'd made out your will or not, whether you planned to remember the Nature Trust, and whether you could say just how generous your intentions were. Chatting with someone about my will was something I'd never done before—nor plan to do again, even with a prince.

125

The next time we met he was tremendously excited about my upcoming visit to China.

"Mrs. Boehm, please. You *must* do me a favor," he said.

"Of course, Prince Bernhard."

"Find out how many pandas there are in China. We want the Chinese to become members of the Trust. Please work on that!"

A few weeks later, when I was in Washington, I met the Chinese ambassador. I bided my time, then after several minutes of friendly chat, I turned the conversation to the subject of pandas.

"Er . . . more or less how many pandas *are* there in China, would you say?"

"Well, really Mrs. Boehm! With millions of mouths to feed, you want me to count pandas!"

Fortunately China now has joined other countries concerned with endangered species. It has become a member of the international World Wildlife Fund, thanks to the sustained efforts and boundless enthusiasm of Prince Bernhard and others devoted to the same cause. Recently, Dr. George Schaller, of the New York Zoological Society, and a group of scientists spent a year in China tracking and studying the life and eating habits of the giant panda in the hope of safeguarding the existence of one of the most beloved animals in the world.

I met "the Prince of the White Carnation," as he was called, several times in the 1970s during his term as president of the World Wildlife Fund. I've always tried to attend that organization's annual functions. One of the more exciting evenings was one held at Harrod's in London in September 1975.

On this occasion, in order to raise monies by auction for the Fund, I donated the last of the three life-size "Mute Swans." The original pair, which was presented to Chairman Mao and the Chinese people in 1972, is in the Great Hall in Peking, China; the second pair is in the West Wing of the White House; it was only fitting that a preservation society should have the remaining pair to use for fund-raising.

Approximately three hundred people attended the elaborate auction and cocktail reception (it was the first time Harrod's had ever had an evening event in their dining room). Advance sealed bids were taken to be opened following the reception; live bidding also was to ensue. The sealed bids, however, revealed an extraordinarily high offer of $150,000; the live bidding did not go as high. The successful bid was placed by an American collector who wanted anonymity and who later requested they be presented by me, as intermediary, to Pope Paul VI and the Vatican Museum. Today they can be viewed in the permanent collection in the library wing of the Vatican Museum next to the incredible Sistine Chapel.

Prince Bernhard, the ever-present white carnation in his lapel, contributed mightily to the evening's success. He managed to greet everyone, smiling warmly and shaking hands. Highly visible, totally engaging, he was the consummate public relations expert.

In the 1980s Prince Bernhard turned over the taxing position as head of the World Wildlife Fund International to Prince Philip of England, who devotes a great deal of time to it today. There is no question about the importance of the cause. The identification and subsequent preservation of our disappearing animal species is something in which we should all be interested.

I first met Prince Philip in November 1971, the day we attended a private exhibition at Asprey's on Bond Street given by Holland & Holland, the gunsmiths. A set of four extraordinary guns with perfectly matched rosewood stocks and handles of silver engraved with pheasants and grouse were being shown to dealers and collectors.

When I was first introduced to the prince, Mr. Asprey told him about the new porcelain studio in Malvern I was establishing.

"My gracious, Mrs. Boehm, I thought we already had sufficient potteries in England . . . but I take it you don't agree?"

Of course I agreed, but I added that I wanted to make *more* beautiful animals, birds, and flowers.

Prince Philip seemed curious. "Which, for instance?"

"Well, sir, bobcats, raccoons, elephants."

"But we haven't any bobcats and raccoons in England, Mrs. Boehm."

"And we don't have elephants in the U.S., but people love them anyway!"

Then we were interrupted. Just as well, I thought. I was, after all, being cheeky with royalty.

Our conversation resumed ten years later, in 1981. The

prince had just become president of the World Wildlife Fund, and I was asked to present him with our life-size porcelain osprey at the Wembly Conference Center.

"I remember our first meeting, Mrs. Boehm," he said, smiling. "What a magnificient bird you have created!" His arms were raised up as if in a gesture of royal approval.

That day, the first osprey made in England brought $34,000 at auction for the Fund. Others were later to be sold in the galleries for $17,500.

I met the prince again in late 1982 during an exciting art auction and black-tie dinner at Sotheby Parke Bernet in To-ronto. For the evening's main event, I had donated to the Fund one of the "American Bald Eagle and Nest" sculptures and provided each of the fifty dinner tables with a small panda sculpture.

I was seated at Prince Philip's table. During the course of the dinner, the chairman announced a surprise silent auction to be held at each table, with the winner taking home the Boehm porcelain panda. A great deal of spirited tableside bidding ensued. An old friend of mine and a great supporter of World Wildlife, John Brogan, won the panda (worth $125 at retail) at his table. He told me he had bid it in for $250 and asked me to sign it.

"Perhaps the prince would sign it, too," he said to me.

When I asked the prince if indeed he would inscribe his name on the porcelain, he answered without hesitating. "Certainly, but only if the bid is raised to one thousand dollars!"

John rolled his eyes heavenward, gasped, and then agreed. Word soon spread that the prince would sign all pandas whose owners were similarly willing to raise their bids to $1,000, and supporters came forward enthusiastically.

What they didn't know was that Prince Philip had a small trick up his sleeve. Naturally the royal family avoids spontane-ous endorsements, especially the use of their signatures for commercial gain. To get around this problem and yet raise needed money for the Fund, Prince Philip cleverly signed each of the pandas with the Greek symbol signifying his name. That evening we both signed seven pandas, which sold for $1,000 each.

27

A Studio in England

"She's the kind of person that even other women like." That comment was made about me when I was being introduced at a luncheon as the guest speaker, and it's the nicest thing that has ever been said about me.

My friendships with both men and women are precious to me, from both an emotional and a spiritual point of view. As I look back at my life, I have an uncanny feeling that many of the big breaks that have occurred in the history of the Boehm company were the accidental result of my personal friendships.

For example, if I had not answered the call of a recently divorced friend who was depressed, and if I had not accompanied her on a quick trip to England, there might not be a Boehm Malvern studio today.

In the summer of 1970 I flew with this friend to spend several days sightseeing and attending the theater in London. We left on little more than a day's notice. I managed to drop in at Thomas Goode's, the great porcelain house, to enjoy a few minutes browsing. There were some pieces that caught my eye, so I asked the managing director, Philip Rayner, about their origin. When he told me that they were made by a small group of young people moonlighting from their Royal Worcester jobs, that was all I needed to hear. I hired a car and driver that afternoon and drove to Malvern, located on the western fringe of the beautiful Cotswold country.

When I walked into their "studio"—a garage that was crudely lit in the evening dusk—I found three married couples working as artisans and consumed with the entrepreneurial spirit. The men—one a designer and platemaker, one a craftsman of green-ware clay as well as a platemaker, and one a painter—felt they would have to wait until they were in their sixties before they could hope to hold top managerial positions in a large British firm. They were full of ambition and the desire to try something on their own, even if it had to be after regular working hours.

Their work was good. It had quality. I decided to move fast. Would they like to join in a new venture?

They would. We held our first board meeting during a picnic lunch near the Wyche Cutting part of the lovely Malvern Hills. It is a breathtakingly beautiful part of England. The new members of our consortium were: Philip Rayner, the three porcelain-makers, Frank Cosentino, and I. I often smile to myself remembering that lovely summer's day when we sat planning and going over the budget, eating cold roast beef, Yorkshire ham, and chocolate cake as we put ourselves officially into business as Boehm of Malvern England Limited.

Our British peers did not particularly appreciate the Americans moving into their field of porcelain. After all, a company like Royal Worcester had monopolized it for over two hundred years in the Worcestershire area. I went to work to make the people in the local area know me and like me. I felt somewhat like a political activist in putting women to work in this depressed area, women who often had been discriminated against. It soon became apparent to everyone that we had created jobs and introduced good benefits for the workers. A second studio on Howsell Road, half a mile down the road from the original one on Tanhouse Lane, was added within the year.

The Americans had landed.

My friendship with the future king of England is something I justifiably treasure. Although I've attended several events with His Royal Highness, my favorite memory is the fiftieth anniversary celebration of the Malvern Festival, honoring George

Bernard Shaw and the composer Edward Elgar, both of whom lived and worked for a time in Malvern. The Malvern Council asked me to act as hostess for the festival.

Prince Charles, the guest of honor at the festival, is particularly fond of Elgar's compositions, several of which were played at his wedding.

It was a great coup for us that the prince's itinerary included a tour of the Boehm studio in Malvern. On a very tight schedule, he was allotted a total of forty-two minutes for the visit. (The British are punctilious and concise in their royal scheduling!)

The prince caught me by surprise by arriving ten minutes early. I was sitting down with my feet up, enjoying a cup of tea, when I heard the sound of several cars outside. I rushed out to greet him just after he alighted from his car, a protocol error on my part. I should have been out there in front, waiting.

He entered the gallery first and signed the visitors' guestbook: "May 20—Charles."

How nice it would be if one could go through life signing a first name only, like a member of royalty!

I toured him through the studio, with my workers hanging on every single word he spoke. The excitement in the place was almost incendiary. He wandered about comfortably from department to department, asking numerous questions of the workers. I wanted to impress upon him the fact that porcelain is very fragile. In the firing room I picked up a tiny unfired clay flower, and with just the slightest movement crushed it into a million pieces. He was shocked. "Mrs. Boehm, that was a beautiful flower!"

"Well, Your Royal Highness, I wanted you to sense the fragility of porcelain-making, in order to understand what a delicate art it is."

I tried to keep Prince Charles on schedule, but he was so obviously enjoying himself that his equerry, Mr. Adean, whispered to me not to hurry but to let him take his time.

When we arrived in the painting division, I asked the prince if he'd like to try his hand at painting the last bit of a baby seal.

"I've never done this type of painting before," he laughed. "I hope I won't spoil it. I'm afraid I'll devalue the piece."

"Not if you sign it, Your Royal Highness," I quipped. The prince chuckled and set about enthusiastically dabbing on some paint.

By now the forty-two minutes had become an hour and a half, and my friend Lady Beauchamp was furious. The prince had been scheduled to change into black tie and have cocktails at her mansion after the tour. Now there would only be time for him to dash in to change and then leave immediately. I was thinking of all the lavish hors d'oeuvres that had been prepared. Lady Beauchamp obviously was not pleased.

That evening I was among the two thousand people who attended the festival concert at the Abbey. Prince Charles followed the entire program with a libretto, tapping his foot in time with the music. I was seated one away from him.

After the concert, in my role of hostess, I introduced the prince to thirty dignitaries—musicians and patrons—before going into the Elgar Suite at the Abbey Hotel for dinner. Prince Charles and I were the last two people to enter the beautiful dining room. As we entered on the long white carpet, everyone in the hall stood in unison. Perhaps I was not supposed to be standing by him. Probably it was a breach of protocol and I was supposed to be *behind* him, but I felt like a queen, anyway.

I had ordered a menu to please His Highness, including his favorite sweet, raspberries Pavlova.

Producing a dessert like this in a small village like Malvern is not an easy matter. The chef fed me raspberries Pavlova for two days, and either the cake was too sticky or the meringue was like gum. We tried everything and finally decided we would have to do a little improvising, so we used a combination of sponge cake and pound cake on the bottom, circled by the meringue and topped with fresh raspberries and whipped cream. It may have been ersatz Pavlova, but Prince Charles devoured every bit of it.

After dinner Prince Charles and I left together and walked to His Highness's car, a two-seater Aston-Martin. He showed me his new touch radio and other automatic features, then buckled himself in and bade me goodnight.

The dashing, charismatic future king of England drove off into the night.

One of the things I like about him is that he is never at a loss for words. He can handle anything spontaneously. I've seen him perform beautifully on several occasions.

At Stoke-on-Trent, for example, he was dedicating a museum in front of a crowd of cheering, screaming girls. Standing behind a rope outside the museum, they were yelling, "We want Charles! We want Charles!" as though he were a rock star. He walked over to them and chatted happily until one of the girls kissed him smack on the lips. He turned slightly rosy and said, "My God, you'll have to learn to control yourself."

It was the perfect remark.

On this same occasion, I remarked on the lovely salmon carnation he wore on his gray striped suit: "Your Highness, it's so beautiful it almost looks like porcelain." (After all, he was at Stoke-on-Trent, the pottery district of England.)

"Well, Mrs. Boehm, I'm afraid not. But if it were, of course, the porcelain would be Boehm."

28

The Unforgettable Chauffeur

Quite naturally, an automobile like my Rolls Royce Phantom VI required a chauffeur to surpass all chauffeurs. Mine was an Englishman—let's call him Rodney (not his real name). There was no one more pretentious than Rodney, a great professional and a superb snob. He loved only VIPs; throughout his lifetime he chauffeured "only for the best, only for the mightiest and the most important," as he himself modestly stated. These included tycoons, internationally famous entertainment figures, nobility—and now Helen Boehm. I no longer merely had to live up to my automobile, I now had to live up to my chauffeur!

In the fall of 1970 I inherited him directly from the Rolls Royce headquarters in Barclay Square. I was recuperating at the time from an eye operation in London, and I had to have a chauffeur drive me temporarily. I liked Rodney's style, so I asked him to work for me on a permanent basis. He drove me all around London and the English countryside.

He was what I would call an "appropriate man," particularly for a Rolls. He was attractive, of medium height, and although he was an inveterate smoker, he smoked only outside the car.

134

Efficiency was his major characteristic. In fact, he was frequently too efficient.

He knew where to go for tea, where not to go for tea, whom to see, whom not to see. He acted as though he were always right and he usually was, but sometimes he was hard to take.

One time a friend of mine was taking me to dinner as his guest. We were going to a new restaurant on Lombardy Street, the "in" spot of the season. Tables were difficult to book. We had heard so much about it, we really looked forward to dining there.

After my friend gave Rodney the name and address of the restaurant, Rodney asked in his haughtiest tone, "Mrs. Boehm, you wouldn't go *there*, would you?"

We didn't. Now there was no possible way we would go there. We went to a restaurant of Rodney's choice.

I kept him in my employ in spite of his rather insufferable superior attitude. He knew about many useful things other than restaurants. His knowledge about ribbons and flowers, for instance, was unequaled.

We were holding a Boehm conference in London one year, followed by a weekend in Malvern. Several hundred people were flying in from all over the world. A few evenings beforehand, I was wrapping the gifts for the ladies: Each was to receive a pink porcelain rose, known as the "Malvern Rose," in a black box. At the last minute I decided to tie a pretty pink ribbon around the box.

"Rodney, I need one hundred yards of pink ribbon right away. I don't know where we can find it at this late hour."

"Madam, do you require rayon-back or satin-back ribbon?"

Within an hour, Rodney returned with the perfect satin-back ribbon.

From then on, I figured Rodney must know everything, but not too long afterward I discovered that even the invincible Rodney could be, shall we say, inaccurate, if not absolutely wrong.

We were preparing the Malvern studio for the weekend guests and I told Rodney I wanted some flowers to add color to the entryway. The problem in the past had been that the birds would eat the flowers as fast as our gardener put them in the soil. Without a moment's hesitation, Rodney was ready with advice.

"Plant cornflower blues, Mrs. Boehm. The birds never touch blue flowers."

The Malvern staff hustled about planting cornflower blues for the next day's open house. They looked spectacular, but by 9 A.M. the following morning, every single flower head had been snapped off! For once Rodney was at a loss for words.

I soon realized that Rodney was given to hyperbole; a good story could be more fun than the absolute truth. Rodney thought nothing, in fact, of inventing a new member of royalty if it suited his purposes. He accomplished this on one of our frequent drives from London to Malvern.

"Mrs. Boehm," said Rodney, pulling the Rolls Royce into a little roadside inn, "this is the proper place for you to have tea today. The tea is blended to perfection here, and the scones are served with the true Devonshire cream and butter."

While I enjoyed my tea, a number of local people gathered around the new Rolls Royce Phantom VI limo, admiringly looking at it from all angles. One old-timer ventured up to Rodney and asked him who owned it.

Looking disdainfully at the entire crowd, Rodney replied, "This car, my good man, belongs to the Duchess of Malvern. It's one of her fifteen cars, and I'm her senior chauffeur."

Rodney's ideas extended to clothes, too.

One day I planned to wear a blue chiffon dress to dinner but discovered I had forgotten to bring my navy blue satin pumps, a fact I mentioned to Rodney. He said not to worry, he would go to Raynes (Delmans) on Old Bond Street to see what they had. Shortly he returned with not one but ten pairs of blue shoes, of which I kept three, one a perfect match for the blue dress I was wearing that night. He had told the store the shoes were for the selection of the Duchess of Malvern, who was staying at the Connaught Hotel. They had called the Connaught and were told, "Mrs. Boehm, oh, yes, indeed!"

Rodney drove me, his Duchess of Malvern, on a trip to the NATO countries in my seven-passenger Phantom VI. A van holding crates of porcelains was attached, and we drove in "stately style" to the American embassies in Paris, Bonn, and

Brussels, where Ed's work was honored in special exhibitions. The star of each exhibit was, of course, the "Mute Swans" piece that was subsequently to be auctioned off in London for the World Wildlife Fund.

The one thing that stands out in my mind about Rodney on that particular trip was his interest in mail.

As we arrived in each new city, the first thing Rodney would do would be to see that I was properly registered, and then he would check the mail—mine and especially his. He always got ten letters to my two, whether we were in Paris, Bonn, or Rome. I never knew why. And he never offered an explanation. I used to make outrageous guesses on what he was up to.

During that long journey of eighteen days, he sometimes drove too fast.

I'd say, "Rodney, let's slow down a bit," and then he would drive five miles per hour, just so I wouldn't make a mistake and ask him to do that again. He really was a good driver, but sometimes he was a bully on the road. Other drivers sometimes made obscene gestures at him. "Oh look, Rodney," I would say innocently, "do you know that fellow who waved so hard at you?"

Nothing intimidated Rodney, not his employer, not other drivers, not even the staff of the White House. My most outrageous Rodney story centers around Tricia Nixon's wedding at the White House. He drove me to Washington from New Jersey and was scheduled to pick me up right after the wedding. I had a speaking engagement in Atlantic City that day, so I had to leave before the reception was over. I told him to park the Phantom VI in a convenient location near the same door I would use to enter the White House.

I attended the wedding and stayed at the reception about an hour. When I came out of the White House, the first thing I saw was my Rolls Royce right at the West Gate, actually *inside* the grounds.

"Rodney, you got the best spot. Everybody else had to park at a distance. How did you do it?"

"Madam, I told them the president assigned me to park right here!"

"You spoke to President Nixon?"

"No ma'am, you're the president, the president of Boehm!"

"Rodney, shame on you."

"Also, madam, I got a wonderful picture of all the security men."

"How, Rodney?"

"Well, they all wanted me to open the bonnet so they could examine the engine. I took their picture while they were all looking inside. I hope you don't mind!"

"But, Rodney, that means they were away from their posts. That's a terrible thing!"

"Oh, but it was only for a second, madam."

I was thankful that neither President Nixon nor a reporter overheard this particular conversation.

Rodney may have perceived me as the Duchess of Malvern, but he was disdainful of all my other employees, even the top executives. This was something I realized only after I had brought him to the United States. The Boehm staff finally rebelled and told me that Rodney must go. I realized that I had to comply, even though he was efficient and loyal to me.

Sadly, I sent him back to England. I saw him in London occasionally after that. The last time I saw him, he had finished driving for the day. I watched from my hotel window as he changed from his driver's cap to an expensive Stetson. Then, with leather briefcase in hand, he sauntered down South Audley Street looking for all the world like a stockbroker!

29

An Unseen Enemy

If you try to think of what it would be like suddenly not to be able to hear or to walk or to see, you would probably become so depressed that you would stop trying to imagine it.

I never thought anything like this would ever happen to me. I was always the healthiest kid on the block all through life, with a tremendous amount of nonstop energy and a plow-ahead philosophy. But then I stepped up to the brink of total despair and the dark world of blindness.

I beat it. I knew God wouldn't let it happen, but I also had two incredible eye surgeons who helped make sure it didn't happen.

My journey in and out of darkness began while looking at property for my new studio in England in September of 1970. One night as I lay in bed in Malvern, I felt a sudden, painful sensation in my left eye. I flicked on the lamp on the bedside table to find some aspirin or some Alka-Seltzer.

My right eye had had limited vision from the time I was a child. My left eye was the healthy one, but suddenly, when I looked squarely at anything with this eye, it felt as though it was serrated, like the edge of a knife. I knew what this sensation meant; during my ten years as an optician at Meyrowitz's, I had learned what this sensation signified. I tried to put it out of my mind.

Feeling terribly frightened, I tossed and turned the rest of the night. Finally, I could stand it no longer. At 5 A.M. I called my dear friend of many years, Algernon Asprey, who was in London.

"Algy, forgive me for calling so early, but I'm in the Cotswolds and a terrible thing has happened to my sight." I then described my condition to him.

"Don't worry, Helen. Just get down to London immediately and I'll see that one of the best ophthalmologists on Harley Street takes care of you. But don't waste any time!"

At nine o'clock I was in the examination chair in a famous surgeon's office. He tried to comfort me and asked me to return the next day for further tests. After a second examination, he patted my hand to soothe me and said, "My dear lady, we must operate at once."

"But you're pointing to the wrong eye," I said. "It's not the right eye that's giving me trouble. I've never had much vision in that eye, but it hasn't changed. It's my left eye, my good eye, that is painful and foggy."

"Mrs. Boehm, we'll talk about that one later."

He then explained that I had a cataract in my right eye and he should operate on it without delay.

The news thoroughly confused me, but he and his colleagues were certain of their findings. I had to trust their diagnosis. The following morning the operation was performed at the London Clinic.

Four days later the famous surgeon removed the thick beige patch from my eye and said, "Helen, I'm going to pass this high-powered lens before your eyes, and then you tell me exactly what you see."

My heart began to pound, probably with fear. I looked directly into the lens and at the doctor.

"Oh," I cried, heartsick. "Doctor, your face is so blurry. I can't believe it." I felt doomed to a terrible fate.

Then he took the lens away. His face was clear as a bell, and from that moment on I could see perfectly with my right eye, the one in which I had had poor vision all my life. It was a miracle.

It was as though the Lord had been saving that eye all those years for me. I prayed that day and I have prayed every day since in gratitude for that eye.

Despite my improved vision, I was not allowed to leave the hospital. It was puzzling, because a team of doctors was holding a hushed consultation near my bed. They stayed a long time. I could hear them whispering and once again feared what it might all mean. It turned out that I had cause to be afraid.

Solemnly, they approached me. The surgeon told me that a shadow on the back of my left eye appeared to be a melanoma, and there were other complications, too. My left eye, the one that pained me so, would have to be removed!

I was stunned, because the future was the worry. What if my right eye, the one that had just been repaired, became foggy again? I would be completely blind! They suggested I get a second opinion in the United States, and he gave me the names of two highly recommended specialists, one in New York and one in Philadelphia.

I recuperated for a month with round-the-clock nursing care at the Connaught Hotel. My two nieces, Francene and Teresa, arrived to keep me company. Francene even brought her four-year-old daughter Lenore with her.

They gave me the courage I needed and helped me build the strength necessary to make the trip back to America and to the ordeal I had waiting there.

I put on a brave act during the day, feeling as though I were earning an Academy Award in the process. At night, after my family left my room, I lay there envisioning a lifetime of darkness and shadows. I worried about my two hundred artists and craftsmen. How would I be able to work with them without seeing? How would I run the business? How would I know if the blue in the bluebird was blue enough? How could I tell if the green foliage was the right shade for that plant?

There were no answers.

When I returned home I went immediately to Philadelphia to consult with Dr. Harold G. Scheie, of the University of Pennsylvania. My dear friends Dr. and Mrs. Ronis (Tillie and Barney) who lived in Philadelphia had helped me before, when Ed died, and I knew they would be there again this time.

After a two-hour examination, Dr. Scheie asked me to return the next day. No decision was made until the third day. The waiting was agony. Finally, he told me—miraculously—that he and his colleagues did not diagnose the problem as a melanoma and saw no reason why the eye should be removed.

I sat in his office crying with relief, unable to speak.

A few days later Dr. Scheie operated on me for a severely detached retina that was causing the ominous shadow on the back of my eye. Ten days later, this gentle yet precise man with a boyish grin told me, "It's a honey of an eye!"

My vision had been saved.

Today I have one good eye for distance and one for reading. Sight is a gift and a miracle, too.

30

A Pilgrimage to the Birthplace of Porcelain

I had to go all the way to China to discover that the word *china* (as in fine china dinnerware) does not exist in that country. *Porcelain* is the only word they understand.

I was probably the first American businesswoman invited to China through official channels as a guest of the government. My journey to the birthplace of porcelain took place when few Westerners as yet had been granted permission to cross into the country that Marco Polo had described seven hundred years before as "the land of silk."

It was indirectly thanks to Richard Nixon that I was invited there. He had presented the "Mute Swans" to Chairman Mao Tse-tung and the People's Republic of China, as well as some smaller porcelains and copies of Frank Cosentino's book on Ed to lesser Chinese officials.

Just a few months later, in May of 1973, I learned that a small delegation from the People's Republic of China was coming to Washington. This made headlines, because diplomatic relations had not yet been established between our two countries. As luck would have it, I was also in Washington at the time of their visit, orchestrating the annual Boehm Conference and Exhibition. (That particular year I had invited six hundred Boehm collectors and friends from around the country.) One of the

143

highlights of our weekend was the dedication by Mrs. Eisenhower of one hundred twenty-five Boehm porcelains that were presented to the Kennedy Center for the Performing Arts by the Delchamps of Mobile, Alabama, and the Lombardos of Jacksonville, Florida.

Why wouldn't the Chinese enjoy visiting the exhibition of Boehm porcelain? I thought to myself. Why not? They were lovers of art. I called Secretary of State Kissinger's office, spoke to his aide, Mr. Solomon, and asked that the invitation be extended. Mr. Solomon was polite and said he would handle it, but I could tell from his voice that there was no chance. He did not know that I always take long shots and often succeed with them.

The next evening, after dinner, I received a message to call Henry Kissinger's office at once. The Chinese had accepted my invitation! Not only that, but they would arrive at my exhibition at Washington's Madison Hotel at eleven the next morning. I started to worry. What would they say to me? What should I say to them? They were not diplomats. They were officials. What kind of small talk do you make with a Communist official who has never been in your country before? Do you discuss the Washington Monument, American foreign policy, or popcorn through an interpreter?

Worrying thoughts about how we would communicate were soon pushed out by worrying thoughts about what to wear. After ten minutes of frustrated activity in my closet, I achieved a momentary calm and selected an innocuous, dignified black and white suit.

On the exact stroke of eleven the next morning, the Chinese appeared, all wearing boxy suits in navy blue or dark gray that looked as though they had come from a rack with minor alterations. Mr. Han Hsu, deputy chief of the liaison office, led the group; the others followed single file. (How different the Chinese diplomats are today, so at home in the United States after eleven years of living here!)

They spoke very little English, but it was enough to get right through to my heart.

"We know about swans," they said, grinning. "Big swans, Mrs. Boehm."

Mr. Han Hsu, who spoke better English than anyone else,

explained that they had all seen the swans in the Great Hall in Peking and had read the book Frank had written on Ed Boehm, many copies of which President Nixon had brought to China.

After looking at all of the porcelains, I offered them a profusion of food and fruit juices, which the State Department had tipped me off they would like. What they loved most of all were the candies and small cakes. There were polite little sounds of joy as they tried each sweet. When it was time to leave, they lined up in front of me and very formally gave me a beautiful box containing a pair of cloisonne vases that were embellished with roses and little birds. I was touched by their gift and also slightly panicked that I had nothing for them. Suddenly the magic number "eight" came to mind. There were eight of them, and I had eight in a series of new bird plates packed into a box. I grabbed the box and handed a plate to each man, saying I hoped it would bring them happiness in their new homes in America.

They did not carry their plates away with them, although I could tell they were absolutely thrilled with their gifts. As I handed each one his plate, he turned and handed it to the man behind him, until finally, the last man was left holding all the plates. Then they marched out as they had entered, in single file.

The Boehm collectors present at this meeting between the Chinese and the Americans were fascinated by the proceedings. They had witnessed a little "porcelain diplomacy" in our nation's capital.

I followed up on the new friendship with the Chinese by continuing to correspond with them. Later Mr. Han Hsu introduced me to the newly arrived first official Chinese ambassador, Huang Chen. Ambassador Chen was an accomplished artist; a well-known book had been written about his work. He played down this side of his life, feeling his job was politics and diplomacy, not art. Nevertheless, there was an instant, strong bond between us.

When I invited the ambassador to visit our studio in Trenton and to have dinner afterward in my home, he accepted. He came in his own car, of course, equipped with his own thermos of hot tea, explaining politely that he treasured his own flavor of tea more than the Western ones.

I was delighted to be able to use the stunning white ivory

chopsticks I had purchased at Harrod's in London the month before. What better guest of honor to use them for than the Chinese ambassador! I served Italian food, which the ambassador had told me he loved, including fettucine Alfredo and *rollatini di vitello.* The ambassador smiled broadly when he picked up his chopsticks, and then he began to giggle. Frank and I couldn't understand his amusement.

"Mrs. Boehm," he said, "what happy news. When were you and Mr. Cosentino married?"

Flustered, I quickly replied, "Mr. Ambassador, we're not married."

"Oh," he said, turning a bright red color. "These chopsticks with their specially painted scenes are reserved for wedding suppers."

I suggested at this point that we all move into the drawing room for some *mai-tais,* but I have been trying ever since to find a bride and groom who would like my chopsticks for their wedding reception.

The Chinese are very gracious about showing their appreciation for gestures made to them. A week later the ambassador's car and driver appeared in my driveway. Out came trays with a hundred eggrolls, complete with cooking instructions.

It was my turn next. I sent the ambassador cuttings from some of Ed's rare azalea plants. Today these very same red and coral bushes flank the entrance to the Chinese embassy in Washington and bloom profusely every spring.

Our warm personal friendship resulted in an official invitation to travel to China, along with two people from the studio. Frank and Maurice Eyeington, the head sculptor, joined me on this incredible voyage to the Far East, an experience none of us will forget. Our mission was to study new and old Chinese porcelain and to serve in an advisory capacity. In 1974 access to China was extremely limited, and businessmen were vying for visas, despite the fact that trade barriers put up by the Chinese were very strict. Businessmen trying to get into China considered our invitation unique.

We landed in Peking on November 29, 1974, and were met by Mr. Hu Hung-fan and Mrs. Chang Hsuch-ling, of the Chinese People's Association for Friendship with Foreign Countries, and also by Mr. Chou Hsin-pei, who would be our guide. Two green sedans called "Shanghais," looking like something out of an old Charlie Chan movie, carried us to the Peking Hotel through the teeming, noisy streets.

Our accommodations were surprisingly good, and the food was delicious. One section in the dining room served Western food, the other Chinese, so we alternated. Frankly, I preferred the Chinese food.

Our itinerary was not for the lazy. We showered at 7 A.M., because that was the only time there was hot water. Our working hours started at 7:30 and ended late at night, with no rest periods whatsoever. Our hosts took us to carpet factories, ivory and jade carving centers, artists' studios, and, of course, porcelain factories. We walked and climbed endlessly to places a car could not take us. We saw hundreds of thousands of teacups. Our hosts asked us our opinion of everything. Of course we knew they wanted praise, but as time went on and we felt more at ease in our surroundings, we began to give them practical marketing and manufacturing advice about products they hoped to export to the United States. We knew we were on delicate ground. We would praise seventy-five percent of the time, offer gentle advice the other twenty-five percent. We certainly did not wish to offend our kind, gentle hosts for any reason.

Everywhere we went I was always greeted by a vice-chairman, never a chairman. I was beginning to feel ever so slightly miffed by never having the chance to meet "the top guy." "Tell me," I said softly to the vice-chairman of the Peking Fine Arts Factory, "where is your chairman today?"

"Mrs. Boehm, Chairman Mao Tse-tung does not greet people at factories. In China, we have only *one* chairman!"

At each factory I would give the vice-chairman a piece of Boehm porcelain. Finally, I ran out, and yet we had another factory to go. In the bottom of my briefcase I found a stray "Honor America" plate with the symbol of freedom, the bald eagle, painted in gold in the center. I handed it to the vice-chairman and he looked at it as though someone had just handed him the Sistine Chapel ceiling. The usually inscrutable Oriental face was full of emotion.

None of us will ever forget the afternoon at the Tangshan

Porcelain Factory when the head sculptor, a man of about seventy or more, begged Maurice, our sculptor, to show him how he worked. Although he did not speak English, he practically forced Maurice to sit down at the work table, and after much arm-waving, we finally understood what he meant.

There we were, thousands of miles from our modern Trenton studios, but there was Maurice back at work in a place that could have been an eighteenth-century room. More than twenty eager Chinese artisans clustered around our six-foot-six artist, who was born in Yorkshire, England, watching every movement of his hands. He modeled a graceful bird for his Far Eastern colleagues, working swiftly with the clay. They applauded when he applied his final touch and turned it over to them. There were no words necessary that afternoon. Art was once again the strongest communicator of all.

As always, there were the children. And the Chinese children were the sweetest, brightest-eyed, most adorable I had ever seen. They followed us wherever we went, like butterflies lighting from flower to flower. At each children's palace we toured, I presented one of them with a porcelain baby panda, and then the children and I played "let's name the panda." The number-one favorite name was Ling-Ling (the name of the female panda in the Washington Zoo, which was a gift from China to the American people).

The children always greeted me with a resounding "Hello, Auntie Helen," a very high-pitched chorus. I would reply in English, but immediately their faces would go blank. "Hello, Auntie Helen" was all they knew, and usually they had spent an entire day before we arrived learning those difficult sounds. I openly wept at one school when a thirty-piece violin orchestra played "Turkey in the Straw," with thirty small faces very serious indeed and concentrating hard on their composition.

The adults in China were always dressed in a drab fashion, in dark sombre colors. The children, on the other hand, were always dressed in rainbow colors—bright blue, red, yellow, and green. How sad it must be to grow up and equate adulthood with a descent into somberness.

My white mink coat was the hit of our whole trip. The children clustered around me, touching it, loving the soft feel.

They sat in my lap and rubbed their faces up and down against the fur. My white mink coat and hat stopped traffic all through China, and I'm delighted that I went against absolutely everyone's advice in taking it. "Oh, Helen, you must dress in a subdued fashion," old China experts warned. "You must never be flashy. It offends them." But since I hoped the Chinese would be natural with me, I felt I should be natural and be myself with them. When I asked the advice of Ambassador Huang, he replied, "Why not be yourself?" Mrs. Nixon, Barbara Bush, and Nancy Kissinger all wore cloth coats on their China trips, so as to be understated. I was determined to be Helen Boehm, and I'm glad.

I'm also glad I had the coat for warmth when we made the traditional visit to the Great Wall. There was a howling ten-mile-an-hour wind; the windchill factor was fifty degrees below zero! Luckily, we were also wearing our pure cashmere long underwear, purchased the day before for only $11 at the Friendship Store. (We did not remove those long johns until we left China. They were an incredible buy, and I felt like sending them to Sears as a suggestion for their next catalog!)

The trip to the Great Wall was one of the great moments in my life. One has to be there to feel the pull of history and the significance of its meaning to the people as a symbol of strength and determination. Chairman Mao had told the young men of China that they would "become men" when they went to the Wall. As an American woman, I too felt the awesome appeal to the winding barricade of those enormous stones on a desolate landscape.

Another place I had always wanted to visit in China was Ching-te-Chen, the ancient capital of porcelain-making, often referred to as "the birthplace of porcelain." Ed and I had often discussed making a pilgrimage to this region. When I requested several months before our trip that Ching-te-Chen be put on our schedule, the request was refused. No Westerner had been allowed to visit the old imperial kilns for half a century.

Our official schedule was changed when we arrived in China; Ching-te-Chen was suddenly added. Upon looking at our group, our hosts had decided that we were tough enough to make the long, grueling trip. (I was no frail, little old lady!)

At times I wondered why I had insisted we go. We spent hours in a small plane and a long, long day in an automobile going over almost impassable mountain dirt roads. In those days no trains or planes went to Ching-te-Chen. There were few stops for tea, and there was no such thing as a ladies' room. A little girl would hold a sheet in front of me somewhere in the bushes, a local substitute for the privacy of a rest room. If it was raining, a woman would hold an umbrella over my head as an additional touch of comfort.

We checked into the tiny Lotus Hotel. I had been waiting many years to see the old imperial kilns, so I did not even unpack. As the cars drove us to the ancient factory, people were lined up ten deep on both sides of the road to see these Westerners. They were amazed by the fact that there was a woman in the group, and a woman with blond hair and a white fur coat at that. The town obviously had been alerted. People snapped pictures with old-fashioned cameras, often inviting me to stand next to them or to be photographed holding their babies. "Helen," Frank said to me, laughing at one point, "would you like to run for office here?"

In the factory I saw row upon row of thousands of dinner plates, cups, saucers, and dishes. I commented to my female guide that I had never seen so much china in my whole life; this was when I learned that *china* to them meant their country and nothing else. I was shown here my first and probably the finest pieces I will ever see of eggshell porcelain. Our guide recited a poem, very humbly and beautifully:

> Fine porcelain must be
> Thin as paper
> White as jade
> Bright as mirror
> Sound like bell.

It was impossible not to think about Marco Polo while touring Ching-te-Chen. It was here he first saw the translucent beauty of porcelain. He was reminded of a seashell, the "genus *porcellana*," hence the name *porcelain*.

If only Ed Boehm had lived to make this trip . . .

It was a sad day for all of us when we left China. We had fallen in love with the country and its people. When all the bags were packed, I assembled the five floor boys who had served as our helpers and maids and handed them a ten-pound box of Turkish Delights. I singled out their leader, whom we'd nicknamed Sam, and said, "We want to thank all of you, Sam, for being so helpful." They had worked hard for us, including affixing stamps on the four thousand postcards we had purchased and mailed to Boehm collectors and friends. There is no glue on Chinese stamps. Sam and his crew attached each one by brushing on liquid glue, laughing and chattering away as they worked hour after hour at this tedious task.

No tipping is allowed in China, so Sam and the boys at first refused my box of Turkish Delights. But after Frank persuaded them that this was a gift, not a tip, they huddled and came to the unanimous decision that they could accept the box. As our car drove us away from the hotel to the airport, I turned back for a final glimpse at the hotel. There were all five boys, smiling, waving, and licking their sticky fingers.

Why is it that in every country the kids are so absolutely wonderful?

Our trip had made news, since we were among the early guests of the Chinese. Upon our return we were besieged by the media, so we gave the press a Chinese breakfast at eight in the morning at the Pierre Hotel in New York. A superb woman Chinese chef moved with her staff into the Pierre kitchens to prepare the food, thus upsetting the permanent occupants to the point of incredible scenes and temper tantrums. We managed to soothe everyone, and the show went on. The authentic breakfast included eggs that were several thousand years old, which turned some of the more hungover reporters a pale green. Everyone valiantly consumed them as well as the other delicious Chinese specialties. The TV news cameras covered my talk, zeroing in on the exquisite gifts our Chinese friends had given us. The reporters lingered, not wanting to leave, loving all our stories about that exotic, faraway land. We were not diplomats; we were artists and business people, so our story was quite different from those of returning State Department negotiators.

I long to go back to China again, but perhaps I have been

unconsciously delaying the trip. It won't be the same. Everyone has new cameras, and they are used to seeing Westerners now. China is a fast-developing country; it has grown more sophisticated in its manufacturing and exporting systems.

I hope, however, that the Great Wall and the children never change.

31

The Vatican and the Missing Turtle

In June of 1976, the great life-sized "Mute Swans" once again entered my life. They brought me to the Vatican, into the presence of Pope Paul VI, whose papacy was ended not long thereafter by his abrupt death.

The anonymous donor who had purchased the "Mute Swans" that I had donated to the World Wildlife Fund International, had asked me to present the sculpture on his behalf to the Vatican. Since he had paid $150,000 for the piece, and since I was anxious to meet the Pope and have this great work of Boehm art in the Vatican Museum, my answer to his request was a quick affirmative.

I flew to Rome on a Boeing 747 jumbo jet with my own entourage of people. The sculpture was painstakingly packed in styrofoam pellets, great care having been taken to protect the fragile base of the composition, a grassy knoll on which tiny flowers bloomed and a delectable little turtle crawled. Accompanying the crated swans were Frank and myself, of course, but we also brought along Frank's daughter, Laura; two of my great nieces, Lenore and Denise; Keith Bufton, director of our studios in England; and Tish Baldrige, who was charged with handling various projects involving our embassy in Rome. Our group, except for Frank, proceeded to the Grand Hotel by limo. As we traveled at a fast clip, the van that had been sent by the Vatican to fetch the sculpture from the airport whizzed by us at an even faster pace, with Frank hanging out the right side and making mock signs of terror at us. (I found out later those gestures had not been entirely in jest; he felt the driver was going exactly fifty miles an hour too fast.) Frank watched closely while the Vatican staff installed the birds on a table in a small anteroom to the private papal audience chamber where the official presentation would take place two days later. He then watched the guard lock the room and turn the key over to the office of the Swiss Guards.

Forty-eight hours later our party assembled in a waiting room before being taken to the Pope's private audience chamber for the presentation ceremony. About fifteen minutes before His Holiness was due to appear, a bishop rushed in with two assistants. He was obviously greatly upset, his eyes flashing with disbelief. Haltingly, he managed to impart the terrible news: "Non è possible, ma la tartaruga . . . la tartaruga, non c'e!" ("It is not possible, but the turtle is missing!").

And indeed it was gone. We entered the room where the swan sculpture had been placed. There was a large white spot in the green grass, made by the thief in breaking the turtle from the base.

It was hard to believe that something had actually been stolen from the Vatican, especially from a locked guarded room.

The incident was all the more ironic, because the turtle is the Italian symbol for good luck.

Naturally, this development was greatly embarrassing to the Vatican. The bishop did not dare forewarn His Holiness. One simply does not go up to a Pope before a presentation at a private audience to inform him that someone in the Vatican has vandalized the gift he is about to recieve. Frank Cosentino saved the day. Minutes before the Pope was scheduled to arrive in our midst, he whipped out a green felt-tip pen from his suit jacket. (He happened to have a green one, the color of cash, because those pens are used by everyone in our company.)

Frank quickly covered over with green penstrokes the white spots where the turtle had been attached to the sculpture. I told the assistants to His Holiness not to be concerned; someday I would return to the Vatican and replace the missing turtle.

And I did—in September 1980, while visiting yet another Pope, Pope John Paul II. Frank Cosentino and I, accompanied by Monsignor Leonard Toomey (pastor of New Jersey's oldest Catholic parish, Sacred Heart in Trenton), quietly positioned the replacement turtle. Afterward we stood for a while in the public hallway while a group of English-speaking tourists came along, listening intently as their tour director described the beautiful objects in that hall, among which, of course, were the "Mute Swans." Unrecognized, we listened to the guide's description, which was incorrect in many of its details. Since shyness is not one of my characteristics, I enthusiastically approached the group, introduced myself to the guard and the tourists, and then told them the real story of the "Mute Swans"—from President Nixon to the World Wildlife Fund auction, ending with the missing turtle, which we had just replaced. I must have taken fifteen minutes with this tale, but there was no way the guide could have stopped me. (It is called the "Don't breathe, keep on talking enthusiastically," Boehm style of lecturing.)

The group applauded when I finished and began chattering excitedly with each other. The guide remained speechless and nonplussed; he looked as though something had just hit him. I long to go back today to listen to the content of the Vatican Museum lecture on the swans!

The mystery of the missing turtle was never solved. I often wonder if the Management Upstairs metes out any special punishment to a person who dares rip off the Holy Father right in his own house!

I also had an opportunity to create a gift of porcelain for Pope John Paul I after Father Yanitelli, a dear friend and president of St. Peter's College, stopped by the Boehm studio one day in Trenton to select a small gift for the Pope. He was planning a visit to Rome in the near future.

Just the week before I had read a touching story in *Connoisseur* magazine entitled "The Gold Papal Rose." It was about an earlier Pope from a small village in Sicily who, shortly after he became Pope, journeyed to his hometown to see his family and friends who helped finance his early years of education in the seminary. To show their love for him, all the parishioners from his first church joined together in a wave of affection and gave him a single gold rose with a deep blue sapphire on one of the petals.

I remembered this lovely tale as Father Yanitelli and I talked. That afternoon I asked the studio artisans to make a simple gold rose for Pope John Paul I, to be embellished with a single diamond.

Today there are twelve Boehm sculptures in the Vatican Museum. I think of them as a lasting tribute to my husband, who in his love of God's flora and fauna had worshipped God in his own special way.

32

Meeting Pope John Paul II

During the trip to the Vatican in 1980, when I replaced the turtle, I was also involved in a unique art exhibition—the first show exclusively of American painters within the walls of the Vatican. It was organized by Terence Cardinal Cooke and the Friends of American Art in Religion. The exhibition covered one hundred fifty years of both modern and traditional American landscape art and included works by Hudson River School painters, as well as by Georgia O'Keefe, Edward Pitt Lawson, Andrew Wyeth, Jackson Pollock, and others. (This organization was a prime mover in persuading the Pope to allow the first collection of Vatican treasures to come to America in 1983, opening first at the Metropolitan Museum of Art in New York.)

Pope John Paul II, a very traditional man, officially opened the "Mirror of Creation" exhibition of American painters. We found it very amusing to watch His Holiness reacting to some of the paintings—the nontraditional, wildly abstract, and expressionistic ones.

As he stopped in front of a large Jackson Pollock canvas, I heard him saying quietly, "Hmm. Well, yes . . . well, very interesting colors." He moved his head up and down in all directions, looking rather quizzically at the zig-zags and splashes

157

of paint, trying to understand them, probably finding them far too removed from Raphael and Leonardo to be enjoyable.

Among those who met the Pope at the exhibition was a dear friend of mine, Jacqueline Goldman. Jacqueline's father, although a French citizen, was born of Austrian parents in Krakow, Poland, where the Pope also was born. After a long internment in a Nazi concentration camp, Jacqueline's father became disillusioned and lost his faith in God. When I related this story to His Holiness, the Pope took Jacqueline's hand and said he and Jacqueline's father had a great bond—Krakow.

After reviewing each piece in the art collection and addressing the assembled group, His Holiness started to leave the gallery. His eyes found Jacqueline Goldman in the crowd and he said, *"Suo padre, suo padre"* ("Your father, your father"), as if to say, "I will not forget him in my prayers."

This cartoon was done with me as Scarlett playing to Clark Gable's Rhett in 1952.

Mamie Eisenhower receives the Boehm porcelain plate "Young America 1776" after cutting the ribbon of the Boehm room at the Kennedy Center in Washington, D.C., in 1973.

Ed with Lady Bird Johnson *(at left)* and me with our "Wood-thrushes"—the official bird of our nation's capital—after presenting them to the White House in 1965.

First Lady Nancy Reagan with friends on board Malcolm Forbes's yacht at 'a luncheon honoring Prince Charles *(Photo © Helen Marcus)*

The Honorable David Bruce, United States ambassador to the United Kingdom, accepts the white porcelain sculpture of the American bald eagle, created for the American embassy in London in memory of President John F. Kennedy, September 1964.

Some of the members of the Horatio Alger Board. *From left:* Dr. Norman Vincent Peale, Arthur Rubloff, John Galbreath, Clement Stone, John Johnson, Charles Lubin. The first woman board member is in the middle!

I present Israeli President Yitzhak Navon and Mrs. Navon with the Boehm porcelain plaque "Seven Kinds," one of the pieces from the Boehm Judaica Collection, November 1978.

With President Anwar El-Sadat after the signing of the Egyptian-Israeli Peace Treaty in 1979

Lord Mountbatten inspects a Boehm porcelain at Neiman-Marcus's "British Fortnight" promotion in Dallas in 1973.

Prince Charles tries his hand at decorating a sculpture in the
Boehm studios at Malvern, May 1979. (*J. M. Mullaney*)

At a reception at Asprey & Co. in London, Algernon Asprey (*at right*) and I chat with Prince Philip. (*John Tarlton*)

As Prince Charles looks on, Princess Diana receives the Boehm porcelain "Victorian Bouquet," representing the flowers from her wedding bouquet, in Saint Mary's Parish Church, Tetbury, England, 1981. (*Peter A. Harding*)

Princess Grace with the first Boehm "Grace de Monaco Rose" at the first International Rose Show of Monte Carlo in June 1981

With Mikhail Baryshnikov, another "natural" wonder
(*Jim Graham*)

In 1977 with famed singers Beverly Sills, general director of the
New York City Opera, and Jerome Hines at the Metropolitan
Opera House with the Boehm sculpture of Miss Sills as "Manon,"
her favorite role.

With H.R.H. Prince Bernhard of the Netherlands *(at right)* and Mr. Midgely, the director of Harrod's, shortly before the "Mute Swans" were auctioned for the World Wildlife Fund in September 1975 *(Photo © 1975 World Wildlife Fund—U.K.)*

In Palm Beach with my good friend and fellow polo enthusiast Merv Griffin *(Lucien Capehart)*

His Holiness Pope John Paul II talks to me at the Vatican Exhibition of American Art in 1980. *(Arturo Mari)*

33

Egypt—The Land of Tutankhamen

In the late seventies, a very young boy greatly influenced the museum world and my own company as well. Only eighteen years old when he died, this boy king was responsible for converting thousands of Americans from a rather lackadaisical, blasé attitude toward museum-going to one of great enthusiasm. The collection from the tomb of the boy king Tutankhamen toured America and drew more people to the museums than ever before, breaking all attendance records.

I became involved in furthering the world's interest in King Tut through Ashraf A. Ghorbal, the Egyptian ambassador to the United States. Long a Boehm porcelain enthusiast, he wrote to me in January 1977 asking if "Boehm might be interested in recreating some of the works of art to commemorate the treasures of Tutankhamen that will be in the United States."

In his letter, Ambassador Ghorbal also suggested he would personally escort me after hours through the exhibition at the National Gallery in Washington. Then perhaps I would want to visit Egypt to "see other aspects of our culture first hand."

It did not take me long to say yes to all three invitations.

Frank Cosentino and I were given a two-hour tour of the exhibition in Washington by Dr. Ibrahim El-Nawawe, First Curator of the Egyptian Museum in Cairo. He explained in great

159

detail the importance of each treasure in the traveling exhibition. Only fifty-five pieces out of five thousand found in the boy
pharaoh's tomb were on view, but it was a magnificent assem-
blage of artifacts.

The decision whether or not to recreate these fine art treasures was a difficult one for me to make. Until then Boehm had
always dealt with nature and not artifacts.

Frank and I discussed it over a period of days. Could we make
the transition from art and nature to figures, jewelry, and other
objects? I didn't know. It also meant we would have to learn the
technique of using pure gold dust.

I succumbed to the boy king. It was impossible to resist the
powerful charisma of this ruler, crowned more than thirty-three
hundred years ago. His appeal to adults and children was equally
strong; his death at age eighteen sealed his place in history
forever, making him a beloved hero for all mankind. When I
studied the touring collection, I was entranced by the mystery of
the collection and by the possibilities of reproducing ancient and
beautiful Egyptian artifacts for everyone.

On May 27, 1977, I flew to Cairo along with Maurice
Eyeington, our head sculptor, and Frank Cosentino. We spent
days in that fascinating land, studying, learning, and ultimately
selecting artifacts for recreation in porcelain.

We were the official guests of the government, and the first
evening in Cairo, Ambassador and Mrs. Ghorbal presented me
with a certificate to this effect. It became our personal pass to an
endless round of adventures.

Before I began my work at the Cairo Museum, I went to the
Abdine Palace to meet with Mrs. Jehan El-Sadat, the First Lady
of Egypt, and presented her with the "Peregrine Falcon," the
great bird of the Middle East. The palace, on an acre of land, is
not large but is extremely beautiful. I felt an immediate respect
for Mrs. Sadat. She is a woman with a social consciousness who
cares about improving the lives of her people. Frank, in writing
about our meeting, described it as an "electric encounter, each
woman feeling the strong presence of the other. Their conversation was open and expressive, two women of the world obviously
relishing each other's thoughts and ideas and all too aware of the
fact that their busy lives would allow them only moments
together."

Our affection has meant that we have continued to see each other through the years. We have joined hands in projects that are committed to furthering equal rights for women.

When Mrs. Sadat told me she was studying at Cairo University toward a Ph.D. in languages and that her final exams were that very evening, I asked, "Will President Sadat introduce you as 'Doctor' after you receive your degree?"

Her dark eyes snapping, the First Lady replied, "Absolutely not!" Women's rights had not gone *that* far.

The display area of the Cairo Museum, which houses items from the pre-dynastic periods, covers nearly five acres. The lighting is poor; the collection is magnificent. Row after row of huge columns and larger-than-life figures greet the visitor on the first floor. The Tut collection is housed on the second floor, and there, in the midst of dust from the centuries, I spent hours with my notebook.

When I peered into the display cases, I recalled the archaeologist Howard Carter's words when he opened the boy king's tomb in 1922: "Gold . . . everywhere the glint of gold." I was moved with reverence and felt I should whisper out of respect for such a magnificent past.

There were nearly five thousand artifacts in that room, and I inspected each one. During the following days, pencil and notebook in hand, Frank, Maurice, and I selected a number of subjects for the Boehm reproductions, including the golden throne, a bird in nest, the god Anubis, a cheetah head, the god Horus, life-sized tomb guards, and a pair of falcons with standards. Then I selected several additional pieces with fascinating stories—obelisks, falcon emblems, a shawabty figure, the goddess Selket and, of course, the magnificent mask of the boy king. Each piece was then photographed, and Maurice made voluminous notes regarding its special features, qualities, and measurements.

Tutankhamen, the last in his famous family line, inherited items from his grandparents, Amenophis III and Tiye, as well as from other relatives. His tomb, one of the smallest of all the pharaohs, contained an amazing array of objects, including four chariots, two life-sized figures of the king, a flotilla of model boats, 116 baskets of fruit, and four thousand other smaller objects. Among the latter were 413 shawabty figures, the carved wooden figures of workers designated to help the king in the next world. Generally the ideal number of shawabtys is 401—one for each day of the year and 36 to direct or manage the workers.

I asked why King Tut had extras. The Egyptologists told me they believe the extra twelve were designated one for each month.

One evening after working at the Cairo Museum, my guide took me to a typical shop called the Egypt Bazaar. It was a business that had been in one family for three generations and was run by Mondey S. El-Gabry. We had a great time bargaining over various items, so that what was designated as a "twenty-minute stop" turned into a two-hour marathon of wheeling, dealing, and laughter.

Among the things Mondey sold were fine inlaid backgammon games. We struck a bargain over one particularly beautiful set: I would pay the marked price if I lost a game, but Mondey, a champion tournament player, would make a gift of the set if he lost.

I won!

By now Mondey and I, in the Egyptian tradition, were fast friends. Kissing me twice on both cheeks, he invited me to his tent in the desert for dinner. Following an old Bedouin custom, Mondey kept a tent for weekends, although he and his wife maintained a Western-style home on the edge of Cairo.

He promised that his wife would prepare a Bedouin dinner, and, in my honor, a well-known belly dancer would perform, as would his white Arabian stallion, the famous Jimmy, who danced and pranced to the sound of steel drums. Both have performed for presidents Nixon, Carter, and Ford, as well as for other American dignitaries.

Mondey and his chauffeur, in a new Mercedes, picked up Frank, Maurice, and me at the Hilton Hotel and drove us to his tent, pitched about a mile behind the Great Pyramid. I expected a regular tent, twenty feet square or so, maybe a little bigger. Nothing could have prepared me for what lay ahead on the quietly shifting white sands.

Mondey's tent was mammoth—at least one hundred feet long and sixty feet wide—and flanking it were two smaller satellite tents, one the kitchen, the other a bathroom complete with flush toilets.

His beautiful wife, Amina, only twenty-four, spoke no English but smiled all the time, a response that results from centuries of tradition as well as necessity. They were married when Amina was only fourteen, and now they had four children.

Because the El-Gabrys are Moslems, they do not drink alcohol, but Mondey arranged for whiskeys and a beer called Stela to be served. He thoughtfully had kept the beer on ice all afternoon, a great luxury in the desert, since ice costs far more than beer in that part of the world.

The tent was softly lit with yellow lamps; its walls were adorned with antique tapestries, and a rich Oriental rug covered the huge wooden floor. Everything was red, orange, yellow, and turquoise. Fourteen musicians played tambourines, flutes, castanets, and other instruments, and while they were playing, Nadia, Egypt's leading belly dancer, burst into the tent. After a sensuous, electrifying performance, she asked Frank and Maurice to dance with her. They willingly tried to dance, but her hips undulated too rapidly, and they could not follow the tempo. The Egyptians laughed and then applauded the two American men, not for their grace but for their good nature and sense of sportsmanship.

Next came Jimmy, the beautiful Arabian stallion, who pranced in time to the music. When his incredible display was over, I decided to get into the act, too. Mondey had casually suggested I take a moonlight ride into the desert on Jimmy, not realizing I would be game—never mind the fact that I had not been on a horse in years. Everyone pleaded with me not to go, but the mood of the evening was exciting, the atmosphere electric, and despite the Egyptian *galabiya* robe I wore (which made mounting a horse extremely difficult), I somehow managed and rode off into the night toward the magnificent Pyramids, with Jimmy's nervous trainer alongside.

My trip to Egypt also included visits to Abu Simbel, Aswan, Philae, Luxor, Karnak, and the Valley of the Kings. But the highlight for me in the glorious land of Tut was my ride on Jimmy.

Our involvement with Egypt continued after our trip. A percentage of the money from the sale of the Boehm Tut porcelain reproductions was given to the Metropolitan Museum of Art and the Cairo Museum through the Egyptian Organization of Antiquities.

And then, in 1979, one hundred seventy Boehm collectors and I returned to Egypt. Each participant on this trip donated $1,000 to the Faith and Hope Medical Center (Wafa Wa Amal), Mrs. Sadat's primary charity, and part to the Crippled Children's Hospital, which the First Lady visited religiously every week.

It was inspiring to watch children's faces light up when Mrs. Sadat entered a room. They clung to her with love and affection, as though she were their own mother. She is one of the world's most remarkable women.

Once again porcelain had afforded me entry into another exciting world. It had opened the ancient doors of Egypt, giving me the honor of knowing such a magnificent and compassionate woman as Mrs. Sadat.

Although my friendship with Mrs. Sadat has been a close one, I did not have the privilege of meeting President Sadat until President Carter held a dinner in honor of the signing of the Camp David accords. The dinner took place on September 18, 1978, just hours after President Sadat had signed the agreement with Israeli Prime Minister Menachem Begin and President Carter.

Ambassador Ghorbal asked me to hurry over to the Egyptian embassy in Washington, D.C., that afternoon on only a moment's notice. I was staying at the Madison Hotel and had just set my wet hair in rollers in preparation for the black-tie dinner honoring the Camp David participants when the telephone rang. It was the ambassador's secretary, saying an embassy car would be coming to fetch me in fifteen minutes. I quickly took my damp hair out of the rollers, brushed it as hard as I could, and grabbed the first thing I came upon in my closet, a black pinstripe suit.

Once at the embassy, I was ushered into a very formal drawing room. President Sadat looked at me and I at him, and we both laughed. We were wearing suits of identical fabric. Then we were introduced, but he was still laughing. "Mrs. Boehm, we are like twins."

I gave him a bas-relief portrait of himself in Boehm porcelain, and he made a little speech in front of all the guests in the drawing room, saying that Boehm had made such an enormous contribution to the Cairo Museum with the sale of our reproductions. "We are grateful to the Boehm Company," he said, "for bringing reproductions of the ancient art of Egypt into American homes."

My hair was still wet when I sat at dinner that night at the White House. No one really noticed, myself included. There were many more important things happening in the world that evening.

We continued to create and sell our Tutankhamen replications for three years, the length of time the ancient collection remained in the United States. We coordinated major exhibitions with our retail representatives and with some of the museums in which the original collection was shown. This experience certainly is among the most important in our studio history of three and a half decades, and the Boehm Tutankamen reproductions, in my opinion, are among the finest porcelains, both technically and artistically, ever to be made.

The complete collection of Boehm Tutankhamen replications is as follows:

Alabaster head	Golden-throne bas-relief
Bird in nest	Gold head
Blue lotus	Guardian figures
Cartouche paperweight	Harpooner
Cedar-throne bas-relief	Small ibis
Cheetah head	Ivory-chest bas-relief
Child king	King on leopard
Child Tutankhamen	The mask
Commemorative plates	Obelisks
Faience cup	Perfume bottles
Falcon emblems	Sacred cowhead
Falcon head	Sacred ibis
God Anubis	Scarab paperweight
Goddess Bastet	Shawabty
Goddess Selket	Votive-shield bas-relief

34

Saudi Arabia—Not for
Men Only

Heart, soul and compassion open all *doors.*

In 1978 it seemed as though
anyone with anything to sell was trekking to the Middle East on
business. The Arabs were also buying art by the carload. I was
convinced this was a market that should be tapped for Boehm
porcelains. I mentioned jokingly to Frank Cosentino one day
that "every home with a splendid Oriental rug should also have a
piece of Boehm." Frank countered that if this were to come to
pass, Boehm production would have to increase ten thou-
sandfold.

My friends pooh-poohed the idea of my making a selling trip
to Saudi Arabia. They told me that even their husbands had
trouble trading with the Saudis and that "an American woman
would never be allowed to transact business for her own company."

They were wrong. In March I flew into Riyadh and twelve
hundred pieces of Boehm porcelain (worth $1,500,000) in
crates left at the same time on another jet. Hundreds of ocean
vessels were lined up ten deep at Jeddah, the country's main
harbor, waiting for clearance before unloading, so I knew it
would be suicidal to ship the porcelains by sea. The Saudi
commercial airlines were not equipped to handle a precious

166

cargo of art, so I did what I had to do—I leased my own 707 cargo jet. You don't have to go to graduate business school to know how to take risks and solve problems.

I was the only woman in First Class on the Saudi jet. The men looked at me curiously. I kept to myself, reading hundreds of pages of briefing papers on the country and chatting occasionally only with the flight attendants. It was a long flight, and this "mystery woman" used the time to learn how to handle herself in this country. A flight attendant told me at one point that a group of men talking over their after-dinner drinks had decided I was a "United States government courier."

My friends Ambassador Ashraf Ghorbal and his wife, Amal, of the Egyptian embassy, had introduced me in Washington to good friends of theirs from Cairo, Mr. and Mrs. Adeli Y. Khalil. Mr. Khalil, a leader of the insecticide and forestry business in Egypt, had subsequently arranged to open doors for me in Saudi Arabia through his contacts in Riyadh, Jeddah, Alkhobar and the American petroleum complex in Dhahran.

It was a lesson in conspicuous consumption at Riyadh International Airport when we gathered our baggage after landing. Families meeting the Saudi passengers collected dishwashers, television sets, electric blenders, microwave ovens, and huge boxes from Nieman Marcus in Dallas and Harrod's in London. I saw inflatable pools being unloaded, as well as comforters, stereo sets, and the familiar blue Tiffany boxes. The inspectors who rummaged through the bags found one bottle of liquor after another and immediately turned them upside down, emptying their contents into special sinks installed just for that purpose. Saudi Arabia's strict laws against alcohol are observed, but I have often wondered whether some smart person hasn't installed containers underneath the sinks to collect the liquor as soon as it is poured out.

The Khalils and some other friends were at the airport to greet me. I was grateful for that, because this was very unfamiliar territory for me. After checking in at the Intercontinental Hotel, my staff and I spent the rest of the day and most of the night checking details on the exhibition that was to open the next day. Someone once asked me what I do about jet lag on these long trips, and I answered, "What's that?" If you're traveling on Boehm business, you have no time to consider something like that. And if you don't have the time to think about it, you don't suffer from it.

In setting up our exhibit of Boehm porcelains, we had to open outdoors in the hotel courtyard several hundred well-packed cartons that had arrived on our chartered cargo plane. Each carton was jammed with styrofoam "peanuts," a light but effective packing material. A wind storm suddenly arose, whisking thousands of the pellets from the open cartons and carrying them miles away into the desert around us. I wondered what the nomads would think when they saw not a sand storm, but a white peanut storm approaching!

During my stay in Saudi Arabia I met many families, and I loved most of all talking to the children. Children are my instant friends in every country; my best memories of every country to which I have traveled have always been of them.

One day I lectured to the women medical students at the Al Faisal Hospital. (In Saudi Arabia, male doctors are not allowed to examine women, so these young female med students were destined to have very important careers in their country.) One of the young women was appointed my personal guide throughout the day. She showed me the classrooms, libraries, and laboratories. Although she wore long somber robes and appeared very serious, my guide had a superb, dry wit. While we were observing anatomy students studying the heart, my friend pushed up the sleeves of her garment, picked up a still-beating large animal heart with her bare hands, and placed it in my own hands. "Here, Mrs. Boehm," she said, "don't drop it!" I almost dropped it on the floor in shock. Ed Boehm would have relished the experience; to me the episode was very unsettling.

I caught the hem of my skirt on a nail that afternoon, and part of my bare leg was exposed. Even though there were only women around, my guide nervously whispered, "Mrs. Boehm, cover your leg at once, please. We might meet a male doctor." Saudi women are never allowed to show arms or legs in front of men outside their family.

At the end of the day I stood on the steps of the school watching the medical students file out, one by one. Each girl dutifully pulled her black veil down over her face as she came through the heavy doors in answer to the call of her name as her car arrived. More than a hundred shiny black Cadillacs, Mercedeses, and Rolls Royces were lined up bumper to bumper, waiting to take the medical students home. Women are not allowed to drive, of course. I thought about the fact that even though many of the customs in this country were alien to Westerners, a part of this particular scene nevertheless seemed familiar. It took me back to my childhood and a memory long forgotten. I remembered my two sisters and my mother meeting me after school in Brooklyn, and I realized with a new sense of awareness that loving and caring for children is a universal concern.

While in Riyadh I also spent time with a group of young male students. A teacher from one of the local art schools had read an advertisement in the Arabic newspaper describing the Boehm exhibition. He brought his class of students, ranging in age from fifteen to eighteen, to the Intercontinental Hotel exhibition "to meet Helen Boehm."

Suddenly I found myself surrounded by forty dark-haired boys. They pressed near me, almost uncomfortably so, in their enthusiam to see their first blond American businesswoman up close.

While they wandered about the exhibition, one of the boys leafed through the Boehm catalog lying on a display table. He pointed to a porcelain figure of a ballerina and asked, "Why didn't you bring these, Mrs. Boehm? They are beautiful." One after another pushed his way forward to gaze at the human figures featured in the color brochure. I had been told by the government liaison offer in Washington that I must not bring human figures into Saudi Arabia. Therefore, the exhibit contained only birds, animals, and flowers.

The boys were very disappointed. They were extremely curious about the human form, not only because they were teenagers but also because they were studying art and wanted to know more about anatomy, a topic that was "off limits."

Among the boys who visited the exhibition was one of the grandchildren of King Khalid. He was most interested in the porcelain birds, and upon seeing the "Peregrine Falcon," he hastened to tell me that the previous day he had practiced the art of falconry with his father, Prince Khalid.

I told the boys to invite their mothers and fathers to the exhibition, too. Because the law did not allow women to appear in public with men, I opened the exhibition one night to women only, not just for the mothers of the art students but for all Saudi women. Not even the Boehm male executives were permitted in the room on that special evening, only my Saudi sisters.

After the women were safely inside the exhibition in the hotel, they removed their somber outer robes and veils. I expected to see equally drab dresses, but instead they were wearing the most exquisite clothes imaginable—French silks, Swiss cottons, and Italian printed silks. Their jewels came from the finest European jewelers; their makeup was impeccably applied in the Western tradition. I learned that Saudi women actually dress for each other because they cannot be seen by men outside their homes. Consequently, they vie with one another to be the best dressed. (They are not too different from competing American women in the affluent suburbs!)

I received a call from Edward Asprey, a friend and family member of the prestigious London firm, who had read in the paper that I was in town. He asked if there was anything he could do for me. I told him yes, that I would love to see the interior design work that his father, Algernon Asprey, had done for the king's palace. That very afternoon he took me to the palace. President Carter had just been there for a summit meeting, but unfortunately he only had been able to stay fourteen hours, which was a great disappointment to the Saudis. They had spent more than ten days (and many thousands of dollars) preparing for his arrival. The room in which the king and his council meet, and where President Carter was received, was the most impressive of all. It was obviously patterned after America's largest and most splendid corporate board rooms. The huge chairs for the representatives of each desert kingdom were arranged around a long table. Edward Asprey explained that all the chairs were the same size, since only leaders of equal importance are called together at any one time.

While in Riyadh I was invited to a gathering of diplomatic wives at our embassy and was introduced to King Faisal's beautiful daughter, Princess Sara. King Faisal, who had been assassinated, also had a number of sons, several of whom had attended the Hun School in Princeton, where I am a board member. I told the princess of my great interest in the school, and the princess later asked me if I would be willing to put on a small show for some of her Saudi women friends. Even though many of them did not speak English, our film on how Boehm porcelain is made was "worth a million words." The princess then invited me to the palace to meet the queen mother and her brother, Prince Bender Faisal, a man of approximately forty years of age. The prince, who had been unable to attend the exhibition at the hotel, suggested that I return to the palace with some of my porcelains. "Come on back, Helen," he said with a perfect American accent, "and bring your 'stuff' with you."

That evening my colleagues, George Barker, Keith Bufton, John Fuller, and I were given a tour of the palace, including the many palatial rooms of the queen mother. The tour ended at the site of Prince Bender's pride and joy, his automobile collection (of course), which included a custom-made Excaliber. I had finally found someone who was more of a car nut than I.

Next on the prince's agenda was the ribbon-cutting ceremony for his new tennis court, followed by a steak cookout, complete with mashed potatoes, in my honor. (It was just a normal night at the palace in Riyadh.)

The plates were partitioned according to the kind of food served. The steak section was large, the potato section slightly smaller, and the peas allotted to the smallest part of the plate. Although the meal was lavish, the dinner service somehow reminded me of campers' plates!

After dinner the handsome prince offered to give me a ride in an early Phantom II from his vintage collection, an offer I could not refuse in spite of the hour—it was two o'clock in the morning. After all, I had raced across the Egyptian desert in the moonlight on an Arab steed at just about this same hour.

A chauffeur helped me into the waiting car, but the prince waved the driver impatiently aside and slid behind the wheel himself. The glistening white Phantom II raced like a flashing streak down the long driveway and around the vast palace grounds. We careened around curves at much too fast a rate of speed, and I knew my three colleagues were waiting anxiously, half fearful, half jealous.

The prince and I finally returned, and we settled down to the business of porcelain. (It was none too soon for my exhausted associates, who do not have my energy.) At two-thirty in the morning, the prince selected several pieces for his mother and sisters and quite a few for his friends. He examined every piece carefully before making his decisions. The total price was, as we say in the vernacular, a big piece of change!

When the negotiations were concluded, Prince Bender told me he would send over the money the next morning. We heard nothing. Feeling very dejected, the Boehm entourage began to check out of the Intercontinental Hotel at six in the evening. As we were loading the baggage into our limo, one of the prince's secretaries walked into the lobby with a blank check signed by Prince Bender. He asked George Barker (he naturally would not ask *me*, a woman) what the total price of the porcelains was; then he filled in the amount in American dollars. This was a show of absolute trust on the prince's part; it was also a cliff-hanging way to do business.

Our next exhibition was in Alkhobar, a city located in the western section of the country, several hundred miles from Riyadh. We were not prepared for what we found there. The buildings reminded us of MIT. The petroleum museum was architecturally awe-inspiring. One felt that this city must be the nerve center of the oil world. I stayed at the Hotel Algosaibi in Alkhobar, which was owned by the Khasaki brothers. The owners were constantly present. Every time I entered the lobby, I saw the four of them, all tremendous in size and dressed in white, perched stiffly on elegant chairs like penguins, drinking tea from the daintiest of cups.

My first evening in Alkhobar, John Kelberer, head of Aramco Oil, invited me to his home. The Aramco compound was exactly like being back in Houston. The houses, even the design of the lawns, were "American style."

Many of the Americans stationed in Dhahran had come to our Riyadh exhibition and had purchased porcelains, so they were already familiar with Boehm. Our American flowers were especially popular, because they reminded them of home. Some of these oil executives had been assigned to Saudi Arabia for as long as five years or more.

In Alkhobar I met the tall, dashing twenty-seven-year old Saudi Prince Bender (of another branch of the royal family), who as a flyer tested military planes for the government. He was a good friend of other flyers at Northrop, the American aerospace corporation, and had come along with them to the Boehm exhibition.

When he saw me that night, he explained that his wife was in Riyadh having a baby. I knew it was a very special thing for him to bring up the subject of his wife (a private part of an Arab's life and a subject not to be brought up by others). I quickly found a porcelain baby bird to give him for his wife. He was so touched by the gift that, right then and there, he clapped his hands for attention and shouted out an invitation to everyone present at the Boehm exhibition to come to his home the following evening for dinner. There were at least a hundred people in the room at the time, and nearly every one of them came to the dinner party the next night.

His palace was opulence personified. Marble floors. Plush carpeting. Sunken living rooms. One whole wall, about thirty feet wide and twenty feet high, was devoted to the most complex stereo system imaginable. Dinner was superb, but the Saudi men did not eat with us. The five of them, including Prince Bender, dressed in long white native robes, stood around a big cauldron of lamb as the guests enjoyed the gourmet dinner of lamb, rice, and other native foods. Keeping their left hands behind their backs, they pulled the lamb off the bone with the right and ate directly from their hands, including the rice, which they formed into little balls with their fingers before putting them into the palm of the hand. (Arabs consider using the left hand an insult.) It was a sight none of us will forget.

After dinner the carpets were rolled back and everyone danced to the sound of Elvis Presley and Frank Sinatra booming throughout the house on Bender's custom stereo set. When Tony Bennett began to sing "I Left My Heart in San Francisco," Prince Bender danced with me, and everyone clapped with pleasure. Americans and Saudi Arabians, Westerners and Middle Easterners are friends on any dance floor.

Jeddah, known also as Embassy City, was to be our final destination. As we moved from place to place in this strange and wonderful country, our porcelain was transported by large lorries. The drivers were flown in from Cairo and often drove at night in order to avoid the tremendous heat of daytime. They took food and huge thermoses of cold drinks with them, riding the long night through and meeting us the next day.

In Jeddah, we stayed at the Meridien Hotel, which is managed by an old friend from the Madison Hotel in Washington, D.C. The manager promised to make me "princess for a night" during our visit. He accomplished this by putting me in King Khalid's eleven-room suite.

I wandered about all night, going from the black-lacquered dining room to the library, from room to room, each one more fabulous than the one before. Sumptuous silk-covered pillows three feet in diameter were scattered in abundance on the floors in every room. The master bathroom was my favorite, with its marble tub the size of an estate swimming pool.

The Boehm exhibition in Jeddah was opened by the American ambassador, Sheldon West, and his daughter and by Ambassador Wilton of the British embassy. The following day, Ambassador West's wife, who had been out of town with her husband, returned to Jeddah and invited me to a luncheon at the residence in order to meet other diplomatic wives. One of the women was Mrs. Siad Fawzia, wife of the governor of Mecca. She later played an important role in my life. The adventure began the very next day.

While in Jeddah, I had inquired around for names of stores selling porcelain. I was told of one called Sultan, run by three women, one of whom was Mrs. Siad Fawzia. Her other partners were a Turkish lady, Mrs. Addham, and Sheik Mohammad Ashmawi's wife, Ellie Ashmawi.

The first thing I saw when I entered the store was a huge pair of Sevres vases worth a quarter of a million dollars. There was priceless silver from all over the world on display, as well as beautiful jewels—exquisite gifts of all kinds.

My business mind immediately snapped to attention. What an oasis this could be for Boehm! A handsome sheik, who was examining a trayful of antique silver spoons, overheard me ask the manager who owned the store.

"Why do you want to know?" he inquired, putting down a large Georgian server. "My wife owns it along with two other women."

I explained to Sheik Mohammed Ashmawi that I wanted to know if the store would be willing to carry some of my porcelains. Sheik Ashmawi immediately got on the phone to his wife.

"Ellie, have lunch ready in an hour. I'm bringing home Helen Boehm from America."

I dismissed my own driver and car and walked down the street with the sheik to his brand-new white Rolls Royce. (I was certainly in the land of the Rollses!) Within minutes we were racing out of the city toward his palatial country house. He telephoned several friends from his car, inviting them to lunch also. Just as we came into the barren desert, we heard strange noises, like a series of pops. I thought it might be a blowout, but instead the car's engine was registering a loud, hot complaint. It finally whimpered to a stop.

Stranded in the desert with the blazing noontime sun upon us, I wondered if we were going to survive the heat, much less arrive at the sheik's home in time for his wife's lunch. Looking at his carefully manicured fingers, I doubted that car-repairing was one of his talents.

"Helen, come on. Let's get out of this damn car. God knows what's become of British engineering."

I didn't know about British engineering, but I did know that if I had to stand outside in the unbearable 105-degree heat, my beautiful silk Halston would soon be a mass of wrinkles. I wondered what happens first when a person has sunstroke.

I need not have worried. The sheik had a telephone in his car. Within minutes another white Rolls Royce, an exact duplicate of the first, magically appeared, purring up to the spot where we waited. Off we raced again to the lunch in my honor. As we quickly covered the miles, I could not help thinking back to another time, to another white Rolls Royce, the one I had brought back from England without Ed's consent. My mind flooded with the memories of the day he had filled it with his beloved birds and fancy fowl in order to cure me of the habit of borrowing his car. But that was many, many years ago, and much had happened since. I only wished Ed could have been with me there, in *that* Rolls Royce.

When we arrived at Mohammed Ashmawi's home, he showed me his world-famous car collection even before we went inside. As the Saudi Arabian dealer for Rolls Royce, his automobiles included seven Rolls Royces, one in every color and style. On the opposite side of his huge garage were just as many Cadillacs. I was sorry I'd bragged to him about my 1937 Phantom III. It seemed so insignificant in comparison to his abundance of riches.

After a sumptuous lunch of fish, meats, and fruit, Mohammed said, "You must come for dinner tonight, Helen, and bring your porcelains with you. I wish I had time to go to the exhibition, but I don't."

I tore back into town in yet another of his Rollses right after lunch, having become rather blasé about the car by now, and spent the rest of the afternoon in less luxurious circumstances, working with my Boehm colleagues, arranging for rental of a van and packing a number of porcelains for Mohammed to consider. George Barker (my vice-president of marketing) and I arrived at the sheik's home at six o'clock, to be greeted by Mohammed and Ellie's two older children, both of whom were driving small gasoline-powered cars around the courtyard at speeds of 20 miles per hour. The Arab passion for automobiles is universal, they will never have problems getting gasoline.

Mohammed was a colorful, influential person who obviously enjoyed every minute of life. He wore beautiful rings on every finger, drove the most expensive cars, and had a hobby of purchasing gadgets. I nicknamed him "the Hurricane," because he moved swiftly and bargained endlessly. His wife, Ellie, an extremely beautiful and charming woman, wore a Paris designer dress with a low decolletage, something Saudi women dared not do. "I'm German," she explained, "and this is my way of dressing."

During cocktails Ellie and Mohammed's four children repeatedly burst into the living room, showing all of their Western toys: records, video games, tapes, movies, Flash Gordon comic books, Osmond records, Apple computers, and more. They had a veritable department store of possessions.

As the evening progressed, George and I became hungrier and hungrier. By eight o'clock we had consumed every morsel of cheese and caviar. And still no dinner. Not until one in the morning did food appear, but when it was served, it was magnificent, an awesome seven-course affair. At each place there was a stack of seven ten-inch dinner plates, one piled on top of another. As the guests finished one course, the top plate was removed to make room for the next serving of food. My mind ran wild. What an area to sell dinnerware!

After dinner the bargaining for porcelain began in earnest. The Saudis believe in "eyeball contact." I had arrived in Saudi Arabia with honest, proper prices, which was a gross error. I should have doubled them, because if I had, I might have received the standard prices for each Boehm piece. I hadn't known that bargaining is a way of life for the Saudis. I found myself sitting on a huge gold cushion on the marble floor of the sheik's library. No other women were present. Just before three in the morning, too tired to continue, I said, "George, you take over." I gave up in order to get to bed. It worked in our favor, because the prices George obtained were closer to the prices we had in mind originally.

Sheik Mohammed was very clever. He knew I couldn't very well repack and ship back to America the huge $35,000 eagle with which he had fallen in love. But I wasn't ready yet to give in on that particular piece. On all the rest I had given "courtesy prices." He suggested that I visit his apartment the next day, a place in the city where he entertains his male friends. The next evening I arrived clutching the eagle, and we finally settled on a figure. We both came out rather well. By that time I had learned that the Saudis not only love to haggle over prices, they also take a four- to five-hour nap in the hot afternoon to prepare for the evening's activities. That evening I was prepared. I was as well rested as he.

I am still in contact with the Ashmawi family, including their son, who attends school in Switzerland.

Although the Arabs initially objected to dealing with a woman in commercial activities, I managed to convince them not only of the quality of my product, but also of the earnestness and the shrewdness of my negotiations. The newspapers found me good copy, too. *El Medinah, The Saudi Arabian Gazette,* the *Arab News,* and *Al Yaum* ran photos and stories on me. One of the headlines proclaimed, "The United States' Porcelain Princess Comes to Saudi Arabia."

Today the Arabs have become more accustomed to Western women invading their world. They are gracious people, but I have a feeling they don't like the intrusion of foreign business-women any more today than they did a decade ago. They are simply learning to accept the inevitable.

35

A Journey to Israel

In 1978 I also went to Israel, a journey that evolved from my trip to Egypt in 1977 to study the King Tut collection as well as from my having been present at the White House signing of the Camp David accords. I felt so in awe at having lived in such an exciting time and having witnessed such a dynamic part of history, I felt Boehm should do something to commemorate it. The special collection I had just put into work on reproductions from King Tut's tomb would represent the Egyptians. Now would also be the appropriate moment to make a Judaica collection as well.

The directors of the Jewish Museum on New York's Fifth Avenue allowed me to reproduce several interesting and very meaningful artifacts brought to America by Jews who had fled Hitler. These formed the core of a selection which included:

Black-eared wheatear with lupine
Commemorative plates
Common quail
Cup of Elijah
Etrog container
"Finding of Moses" bas-relief
Hanukkah lamps
Fledgling hoopoe
Hoopoe with Sabra cactus

"Keeper of the Vines" bas-relief
"Land of Milk and Honey" bas-relief
Mezuzah, gold
Mezuzah and case
"Our Tree of Life" bas-relief
Sabra cactus
Seder plate
"Seven Kinds" bas-relief
"Simcha" cup
"Song of Songs" bas-relief
"Star of David" tankard

The object I loved the most was a graceful and charming little Hanukkah lamp. Many others must have felt the same way, for it sold out immediately. I gave a percentage of each sale of the museum recreations to the national organization of Hadassah.

The Judaica porcelain collection generated so much interest that I decided to organize a trip to Israel for Boehm collectors and friends. We scheduled it to take place just three weeks after my return from Saudi Arabia. I had come home with another serious eye infection, unfortunately, and this problem, combined with my recent surgery, worried me about making a trip to Israel. Dr. Scheie put me at ease. "Go, Helen, and don't be worried," he said. "Remember, too, that the Hadassah Hospital on Mount Scopus is one of the finest in the world. If you need care, you'll get the best."

One hundred and seventy people joined me on our long flight to the Holy Land. Two Boehm collections for presentations accompanied us. One collection was destined for the Israel Museum in Jerusalem, the other for the Tel Aviv Museum.

We flew on El Al Israel Airlines. Security was extremely rigorous, but our spirits were high. When we landed in Jerusalem, a warm welcome awaited us. It was a fascinating experience, because wherever we went, East joined West, Christian joined Jew, kosher joined nonkosher. As a Christian, I wanted to see the birthplace of Jesus. And I wanted to go to the Mount of Olives. The trip reinforced my own Catholic faith, but I also grew to understand what this land means to those of non-Christian faiths.

My eyes continued to worry me. I went almost daily to the Hadassah Eye Clinic, accompanied by two caring friends, Arthur Rubloff of Chicago and Mary Taylor (who married each other following the trip).

When our group visited the Wailing Wall, my traveling companions showed their love and concern for me by placing messages on the wall asking God to protect my eyes. Whether it was those prayers, the medicine and care given by the Hadassah Eye Clinic, or a nice combination of both, my eye infection healed.

During the trip the first wedding ever to take place in Israel between members of the Mormon faith was held. The ceremony rejoined two Boehm collectors from Phoenix, Arizona—Sandra Olson and Darrel Olson—who had been married, produced six children, and had divorced. The ceremony took place in the Jerusalem Hilton, where we were all staying. Gifts were hurriedly purchased and wrapped, a special large room was prepared for the wedding, and members of the press joined the other guests. I was matron of honor, George Barker of my staff served as best man, and all the Boehm travelers were guests. There was a healthy amount of sniffling when the couple recited their vows.

During our stay in Jerusalem, twenty-three of my group were invited to join me in meeting President and Mrs. Navon at the presidential residence. I presented them on this occasion with several sculptures from the Boehm Judaica collection for the official residence. The Navons were struck by the crossing of the centuries in these objects, copies of treasures found centuries ago in this land, sent to a museum in America from Germany, reproduced by an American company, and now returned to Israel to reside in the home of the head of state.

One of the highlights of our trip was when everyone slept at a kibbutz. This was quite a new experience for many of the group, accustomed as they were to total luxury, now suddenly roughing it in the Israeli countryside. The young people made us feel at home, asking us to share their food and inviting us to sing and dance with them after supper. I looked at those young faces and strong, muscled arms so accustomed to holding weapons and felt terribly sad. If only there was peace in this land, these young people would be engaged in far happier pursuits. That night, when we prayed for peace, there was an earnestness in the Americans' voices that moved our Israeli hosts. It was a night none of us will forget.

Our American ambassador to Israel at the time, Ambassador Samuel Lewis, was amused by the social schedule of our group. He remarked that he never attended black-tie functions in Tel Aviv, but with the Boehm group in town, "I have worn my dinner jacket twice in one week. You Boehm people enjoy yourselves and each other," he said to me at our farewell ball. "I've never seen anything like it."

That last night a group of my friends sang a song to me they had written specially for the occasion. It was corny and wonderful. If you had drunk a couple of glasses of wine before hearing them sing, as I had, you would have thought it was a Metropolitan Opera sextette performing.

To Helen

Helen, Helen, we are thinking
What a plucky gal you are!
Even though your eyes are blinking,
You have led us near and far.

Beauty you have shown to many
With your gorgeous works of art;
All the while your smile is sunny
And you give straight from your heart.

Presidents of state and others—
Our ambassador and wife,
Mayors, artists, and kibbutzim—
Each will love you all his life.

We're so thankful we're included;
On this trip we've learned so much.
We have made new friends with whom we'll
Always try to keep in touch.

Now we're going home to ponder
All the great things we have seen.
For you we are even fonder.
Shalom, Helen—"Porcelain Queen!"

Once again porcelain had been the bridge between peoples of different nations, because our trip to Israel had been shared by many different faiths.

Years later in 1983 we put into work the design of a beautiful porcelain "Dove of Peace" under the aegis of the Biblical and Contemporary Arts Association. The hallmark on the bottom of each piece is the spirit of ecumenism at its best. It explains that "The Dove of Peace" was "created to honor and support *The Living Tree,* a presentation in sound and light of the life of Jesus at the Mount of Olives, Jerusalem, sponsored by the Biblical and Contemporary Arts Association." The piece was made to commemorate 1983 as the "Year of the Bible."

36

The Ultimate Acquisition: A Polo Team

$\mathcal{S}$urely a psychiatrist would enjoy analyzing why I purchased half interest in a polo team. Polo is so fast, so macho, and so symbolically allied to wealth and social position.

I don't need their learned analysis. I understand very well why the Boehm Team came about. Everyone has his or her symbol of ultimate personal success. For some people, it is yachts, mansions, jewels, or great works of art. For me, it is horses. The acquisition of a polo team was for me the ultimate luxury and proof of success in everything Ed Boehm and I had worked so hard to achieve. Ed often disapproved of my luxury purchases, but I know he would have approved of this one because it involved horses.

When that team entered my life, I felt an enormous exhilaration at being involved in such a magnificent effort involving both man and horse. There was also the immense feeling of satisfaction that lifetime dreams *are* realizable. During the years I owned the Boehm Team, I was as passionately interested in this ancient sport as anyone has ever been, and I include in that statement the Indian maharajahs who began the sport.

When I was a little girl, my favorite animal was the horse. I wanted to own one since I first saw pictures of them in my books.

183

I talked about owning a horse when other little girls my age were longing for Shirley Temple dolls. The fact that my parents couldn't afford either a horse or a Shirley Temple doll was immaterial. I read every book I could find on horses. I dreamt continually that I was riding one in the moonlight—a dream charged with grown-up symbolism I never could have understood at that age. Incredibly, that recurring dream became reality almost half a century later in the Egyptian desert when I rode off on an Arabian stallion in the moonlight near the Pyramids.

During the war I had fallen in love with Ed Boehm when he took me riding in Pawling, New York. When I saw the way he rode and the way he could sculpt horses, I knew this man shared my own strong love for the animal. During our marriage many of our happiest hours were spent on horseback or tending to our horses. As Ed's fame and fortune grew, so did our racing stables in New Jersey. Remembering our early days watching polo on Long Island, I once said to Ed, "Wouldn't it be terrific if we owned our own polo team some day? I mean, wouldn't *that* be incredible?"

Ed answered me that day in his usual cryptic fashion: "If someone ever gives a prize for unrealistic dreaming, Helen, you'd win it every year." It was the end of the discussion.

After Ed died, I had no choice but to reduce the heavy responsibilities of managing the estate in order to tend to the business. Every step of disbanding what Ed had so joyously built up, collected, and nurtured hurt me and almost haunted me. First, I sold off the herd of cattle. Then I presented Ed's incredible collection of birds to five of the world's major zoos. The zoo directors' appreciation was so heartwarming that it helped lessen my loss.

Finally, *ten and a half* years after Ed's death, I found the care and racing of horses too much to handle and too reminiscent of Ed. I sold them. Quite obviously my lack of involvement with horses did not last very long, for in January of 1981 I acquired a part sponsorship in the Palm Beach Polo Team from William Ylvisaker, the ambitious, hard-working head of Gould Industries in Chicago. Bill, a tanned, fit, handsome man, had been captain of the polo team at Yale and in private life had played polo all over the world—Iran, Saudi Arabia, the United Kingdom, and other countries. Bill was known for his excellent team spirit, but he also liked to win, two characteristics that really appealed to me. Bill had heard whisperings on the polo circuit that I was interested in polo, so one day he invited me to lunch at the Palm Beach Polo and Country Club (which he had founded).

We hit it off instantly. The chemistry was right, and we closed our deal over one short meal at the club. We managed to iron out all details and shake hands during the amount of time it took to consume our chef's salads. I don't believe in wasting time. I make an important business decision with the same rapidity as an artistic decision concerning a porcelain sculpture design. If I had spent time reflecting over all my decisions, I calculate it would have taken me sixty years to reach the point I attained in thirty.

I have always had good instincts about people, both men and women. Bill was a good decision. We settled on a name for the team, one that pleased me very much: the Boehm Palm Beach Team. It helped people learn how to pronounce my name, because the pronunciation of *Boehm* in this country rhymes with *team*.

The electric Ylvisaker-Boehm energy worked on both the players and the horses, for they became instant winners—first the important Rolex Gold Cup and then the World Cup. During their second season, the team lost only once and that, ironically, was when I was not with them. I was in Hollywood taping the Merv Griffin television show. Obviously "my boys" needed me cheering them on. I managed to make every game for the rest of the season, and they did not lose again.

By now the Boehm Team was "hot." I was invited to start a team in England for five tournaments and for the Queen's Cup competition, one of the highest honors a team can attain. Of course, I accepted.

Prince Charles and I had discussed the Queen's Cup a year earlier when we'd talked during a ceremony in Worcester, England. I told him of my ambition to win the Queen's Cup, and the prince cautioned, "Mrs. Boehm, you'll never do it without at least two British players on the team." I think he was secretly amused at my audacity.

It was a piece of advice I decided to heed. My teammates and I began to search for the best British players we could find, and we were successful. Howard Hipwood and Lord Patrick Beresford joined the team and went on to victory on their own country's turf when we captured the Queen's Cup.

My love for polo was not a casual whim. I wanted to lift the sport from being a "rich man's fancy" to a sport understood and enjoyed by people everywhere. I am certainly not the prototype of the "playboy" polo team owner, but a hard-working woman executive whom the players, the ticket-takers, and the grooms greet affectionately with "Hello, Mrs. Boehm." The fact that I know all their names and talk to all of them is an important part of our relationships.

One of the most fascinating aspects of polo is its history. It is an ancient sport, delightfully depicted in the Rajput school of painting. Rajahs are portrayed playing the game with determination on fields blooming with beautiful flowers.

In 1983 young Billy Ylvisaker, Jr., a member of the Boehm Palm Beach Team, tragically died, so the following year I became a sponsor of "The Boehm International Challenge Cup for Young Professionals." I used a Paul Storr antique (1830) silver trophy as the cup, a magnificent object on a lapis lazuli base, which is kept on display at the University of Virginia, where Billy, Jr., had studied. The cup for young players is dedicated to him, because he represented the spirit of youth in polo.

The 1984 Boehm Polo Team was made up of two sets of brothers: the Hipwoods from England, Julian (rated 9) and Howard (9), and the Gracidas of Mexico, Memo (10) and Carlos (8).

Because of Julian's injury while playing, another Mexican high goal star, Antonio Herrera (9), was flown in from Argentina for the finals. On Easter Sunday, April 15, the Boehm Team captured the World Cup for an unprecedented third time.

The following telegram came from Buckingham Palace:

> I was delighted to hear of your successful hat trick. Many congratulations to the energetic patroness.
>
> Charles

This made the victory even more meaningful. A month and a half after the joy and excitement of receiving this congratulatory telegram from H. R. H. Prince Charles, we met again at Sutton Place, the home of Paul Getty, at the United World College Ball. As we danced over the ballroom floor, we recapped the World Cup game, chukkar by chukkar.

I guess horses are increasingly on my mind, as I am now involved in thoroughbred breeding with Bill Ylvisaker, Sr., and a few other horse friends, such as Clay Camp and John Finney. Our brood mare stock is excellent and sure to drop some great champions, possibly a Kentucky Derby winner that goes on to the Triple Crown or a $1 million Budweiser winner in Arlington, Illinois.

The horse is in my opinion the eighth wonder of the world. It has figured as man's great friend and servant since the earliest of civilizations. Artists have always loved and honored it, as we can see in the Ming and Tang horse statues, the Roman equestrian statues, the Etruscan murals, and all through the world of art.

My ambition in life is to be less busy and to spend less time around people and more time around horses, which an old cowboy out West told me one day was the sign of mature judgment.

37

A Royal English Weekend

Because of my deep love for young people, I have always been interested in helping educational causes. I have never had any children of my own, but I have been deeply connected with my family members' children and my friends' children, and there has always been enough energy left over to help raise money for orphanages, schools, children's hospitals, and scholarship programs.

I have watched the rise in creativity in fund-raising over the last twenty years with great fascination. Someone always seems to come up with a new idea to spark people's interest, just when the usual charity benefit begins to pall.

Late in 1981 some friends and I decided to help Prince Charles with his pet charity, the United World College Schools, which was about to celebrate its twentieth anniversary and was in great need of funds. We conceived of a plan to build an entire weekend—the weekend of Memorial Day 1982—around an unbeatable combination: English royalty, polo, parties, and the grandest of balls to be held on one of England's most famous estates.

Prince Charles, an avid polo player like his father, Prince Philip, became involved with the United World College Foundation through his favorite uncle, Lord Mountbatten of Burma,

188

a founding spirit of the organization. Today, there are six schools within this group—in Wales, Canada, Singapore, Swaziland, Italy, and the United States—all founded on the premise that "the quality of the individual outweighs national differences." The aim of these schools is to promote international under-standing in young people during two of the most impressionable years of their lives, the last two years of high school.

Although Prince Charles had been connected with United World College since 1978, he became adamantly committed to his uncle's project when Lord Mountbatten was tragically killed in a terrorists' plot.

Anyone who knew Lord Mountbatten was smitten by him. When he was in the United States trying to raise funds for the United World College Schools in 1972, I introduced him to Stanley Marcus of Neiman-Marcus, which resulted in a very successful ball held in Dallas to benefit the school. During that Dallas visit I purchased at auction the only replica of the precious Cardinal Wolsey Gold Cup, which had been in the Mountbatten family collection for generations. It was a major expense for me, but if there was ever a person who could outsell me, it was dashing Lord Mountbatten. I succumbed to his sales pitch and later donated it back to the United World Colleges for auction during our big English weekend Memorial Day of 1982.

That weekend turned out to be a fund-raiser's dream ($1.7 million raised for the charity) and a society columnist's fantasy (the press carried lavish reports of it in fourteen countries). We christened our weekend festivities "The Polo Weekend." It consisted of a Friday night fashion show and dinner, given by Dr. Aldo Gucci in the majestic Guildhall of London; a Saturday night dinner dance hosted by Lord and Lady Romsey at Broadlands (the 1700-acre country estate that had belonged to Lord Mountbatten); and the first round of play for the Queen's Cup in polo on Sunday.

I persuaded the other organizing committee members to reserve rooms in the luxurious Dorchester Hotel for the Ameri-can weekend participants. If they were going to spend a lot of money on this trip, they should be pampered in elegant sur-roundings. It was part of the spirit of the weekend.

On Friday night approximately five hundred Americans and

English friends gathered for cocktails in Guildhall, parts of which date back to the fifteenth century. Aldo Gucci, our host, was well known for his use of show business techniques in presenting his collection, and he did not disappoint us. The models showed his new fall line during the cocktail hour against a stage background depicting the Orient Express train and to the fast beat of Italian rock music. Then we were served dinner in the very room where Lady Jane Grey had stood in the dock to hear her sentence, but it was hard to empathize with Lady Jane while the waiters were serving vichysoisse, pancakes filled with scampi in lobster sauce, piccata of veal gratinée with white wine sauce and sliced mushrooms, spinach with pine nuts, courgettes, Jersey potatoes, carmelized oranges for dessert, with sponge fingers, fresh fruit, coffee, and then a little port and brandy.

Between the entrée and the dessert, the lights suddenly went out and we were plunged into an eerie velvet darkness. Then a spotlight illuminated a statuesque blond model dressed only in a black leotard and a blazing diamond necklace. She was followed by a succession of other beautiful young women modeling diamonds, one of which was to be auctioned off at the Broadlands Ball the next evening. The women guests all strained to see the jewels perfectly; the men strained to see the models perfectly. I heard one of the men at our table complaining with a twinkle in his eyes, "If I look any harder at the girls, I'm in trouble with my wife. If I look any harder at the jewelry, I'm in worse trouble with her; she might make me buy something."

On Saturday night we put our spirits into full gear with a cocktail party at the Dorchester. Dressed in full-blown evening regalia, the entire group sallied forth from the hotel into chartered buses that were to take us to the quaint village of Romsey, not far from Southampton. I had to be at Broadlands ahead of time to attend a small reception hosted by Prince Charles for the hard-working chairmen and patrons, so I traveled by private car. The bus passengers hardly complained. Arrangements had been made for comfortable, air-conditioned coaches; each pair of seats was equipped with its own table, drink tray, and napkins. Pretty hostesses served champagne and caviar throughout the trip.

The ride to Romsey through the beautiful English country-side, dotted with grazing cattle, sleepy sheep, and stately homes looming beyond thatched-roof villages, took a little more than two hours. I stared at the passing scenery, thinking to myself how fortunate I was, and somehow I felt Mama and Papa were aware of all of this, too, sharing in my excitement.

My hair had been put up in a French twist, and I had chosen a black taffeta Caroline Herrera ball gown with white puff sleeves and tiers of ruffles forming a billowing skirt. The competition tonight would be very tough, I knew, but I felt as well dressed as anyone there. My emeralds and diamonds would hold their own against the antique and ancestral jewels on the royals and peers who were attending the evening's event. By the time the American guests had arrived, most of the British guests were already there; their Bentleys, Jaguars, and Rolls Royces filled the sweeping driveway in rows, their chauffeurs waiting patiently alongside.

The Americans walked from the buses two by two in solemn procession up to the recessed portico of the great Broadlands mansion. I joined them at this point. I'm sure we shared a feeling that we were stepping into a part of England's history as we entered the magnificent hall with its octagonal dome. Someone said, "Look up," so we all did, to view an elaborate ceiling of the most delicate plasterwork in a design of snow-flakes. Lining the hall were priceless marble sculptures from ancient Greece and Rome, acquired by a former owner of Broadlands, Henry Temple II, during his obligatory grand tour of Europe in 1765 as a young man. We walked past these statues with reverence, as we were in a very special kind of museum. This splendid house, one of the finest examples of mid-Georgian architecture in England, has always been a favorite of the royal family. Queen Elizabeth and Prince Philip spent part of their honeymoon there, as did Prince Charles and Princess Diana. Prince Charles was best man at Lord Romsey's wedding, which was performed in the Broadlands chapel.

The clusters of guests were now being organized to pass through the receiving line. We were ushered across the parquet floor of the library and then out of that room into the large salon. Each guest's name was called out in a resounding tone by the official announcer of the royal court as he or she stepped up to greet the Prince of Wales and his beautiful blond wife, Princess Diana, who wore an iridescent red taffeta gown, cut low in front, with the large puffy sleeves that were the fashion of that season. I couldn't help noticing her lovely skin and deep blue eyes. A diamond necklace with a sapphire pendant much larger than her engagement ring stone rested on her chest. Everyone in the receiving line seemed transfixed, but she seemed relaxed in spite of our undisguised staring.

Next to the royal couple stood Lord and Lady Romsey, our handsome young hosts for the evening. Lord Romsey (the Honourable Norton Knatchbull), in his early thirties, is one of Lord Mountbatten's grandchildren. He and his striking wife, Penelope, live at Broadlands with their son, Nicholas, who at this point was only a year old. The slender Lady Romsey, her long golden hair swept up into an elaborate hairstyle, looked as though she'd stepped out of a Gainsborough painting.

The receiving line moved far too quickly. Each guest suddenly found him- or herself being escorted through the tall French doors onto steps leading down to a spectacular sweep of green lawns. The carefully manicured grass led in turn to a winding river, the Test, where the sun, now a subtle shade of salmon, was just preparing a spectacular sunset over the quiet water.

Waitresses in black with white aprons and caps filled crystal glasses with champagne. The Americans, generally unfamiliar with meeting "the royals," began to relax. The Prince of Wales strolled amoung us, chatting and sipping champagne.

I heard some whispers behind me and suddenly realized I was being discussed.

"Do you know her?"

"I've always wanted to meet her, ever since my mother began collecting her porcelains."

I was enchanted, feeling quite like a celebrity. A normal person might pretend not to hear that conversation, but reticence has never been my strong suit.

"I didn't mean to be overhearing something I shouldn't, but I did hear what you just said."

The young woman blushed and said in a clipped English accent, "Oh, Mrs. Boehm, I'm delighted to meet you. My mother was married to an American and lived in the States until 1970. She was one of your earliest collectors."

"How nice of you to tell me that," I said, secretly thinking how pleasant it was to have an English woman tell me that her English mother collected Ed's porcelains instead of Dorothy Doughty's or those of the other great English ceramicists who'd begun decades before Ed did.

We were soon ushered into a giant pink and white striped tent for dinner. The tent ceiling was draped in pink chiffon on the interior, which in the candlelight cast a flattering pink glow on everyone's skin. Even men look better when women look better! Each of the forty-five tables of ten was covered with a rose tablecloth and had a basket of fresh flowers in the center. The flowers looked like a bouquet just plucked from a nineteenth-century English garden. I could not keep my eyes off them. One person at each table would win a long-stemmed "Lord Mount-batten Rose" of Boehm porcelain in a silver vase, my gift for the evening.

The master of ceremonies announced that those guests with a cross on their dinner programs were the winners of the rose. There was much excitement while the programs were checked, and at the evening's end, forty-five happy people departed with silver vase and rose in hand, a beautiful memento of the ball.

At one table there were ardent Boehm collectors who had previously traveled with me on trips I had organized to Israel and Egypt. "I just wish she would organize more of these events," I overheard Mrs. Alta Faubus, widow of the former governor of Arkansas, telling her dinner partner. "They are expensive but so worthwhile."

Frank Feggle, from Los Angeles, explained to everyone at his table that he attended as many of my sponsored events as possible because, "they're always so lively. Helen doesn't know how to put on a dull party. And, also, our money goes to a worthy cause." One couple had even marched to the altar because of my trips. Kate Smith and Larry Gilman, who had met on the Egyptian journey, were subsequently married and had joined us for this evening at Broadlands.

Shortly after everyone was seated, we were called to atten-tion. Everyone rose; the tent was quiet. The prince and princess, accompanied by Lord and Lady Romsey, came in through a side entrance of the tent and walked to the center tables, where they took their places for dinner. Rather than putting them all together at one head table, our committee had decided to share "the royals." Each one was placed at a separate table so that as many guests as possible would be able to visit with them.

Dr. Armand Hammer and I were privileged to sit with Princess Diana. Chatting about polo, the princess confessed to me that she was "just beginning to understand and enjoy it." She admitted that she did not come from a "horse background," but she tried to attend every important game, even when the temperature reached eighty-eight degrees, which by English standards is "too beastly hot for any civilized activity."

I, in turn, shared with her the story of how I had come to love this exciting sport. "It's like ballet on horseback," I told the princess. "I became involved only after racing horses in America for many years. You will find that the more you watch it and learn about it, the more exciting it becomes. It is an art form."

In the middle of the salad course, Diana suddenly reached over and admiringly touched the emerald ring on my hand. "You have an excellent eye for fine things," I said, laughing. Then I removed my ring and handed it to the princess. "Here, do try it on."

The princess, her eyes dancing with mischievousness as she slipped it on, quickly hid her hand under the tablecloth and said to me, "Good-bye now, Helen Boehm!"

Everyone at our table was impressed by the princess's sense of humor and good nature. The rest of us were so much older. She must have found it rough sledding, but one would never have known. Not even thick cigar smoke ruffled her. Toward the end of the dinner, the waiters passed cigars to the gentlemen, and one of the men nearby began smoking. The smoke irritated my eyes. Sensing the discomfort it must be causing the princess (who was expecting her first child very soon), I began to fan the smoke away from her with my dinner menu.

The faster I fanned, the faster the smoker puffed. Finally, perhaps glimpsing my frank disapproval, he put out his burning cigar but did it in a glass of wine! The princess and I exchanged glances and bit our lips in order to avoid laughing out loud and embarrassing him. The princess rolled her eyes heavenward in a glance at me as if to say, "There's not much hope for *some* people."

Shortly after he sat down, the prince noticed that one place at his table was empty. When no one came, he summoned one of his guards from Scotland Yard and asked him to find out what had happened to the missing person. He was concerned that someone was ill or had been in an accident. He was soon reassured that it was merely a seating mix-up. Since I had been involved in seating the dinner, I was mortified. Well, it was too late. The empty seat remained, and I never looked at the seating charts later to find out what had happened. I preferred not to know.

The dinner began with smoked salmon and white wine. After the second course of "Supreme de Volaille Broadlands" was served, the musicians were given the signal to play, and the dancing started. Perhaps in honor of the Americans, many of the tunes were familiar old favorites—"Sweet Georgia Brown," "I've Got You Under My Skin," "That Certain Feeling." It was sedate, to say the least. No hint of British rock tonight!

Lord Romsey temporarily halted the dining and dancing just before the strawberries with clotted Devon cream were served. He made a few welcoming comments and then turned the microphone over to his old school chum, Prince Charles.

The guests sat attentively, waiting to see what kind of public speaker Charles was. They found out quickly that he is superb. He began by telling the audience he was "absolutely amazed to discover while chatting about during the champagne hour that many of you do not know very much, if anything, about the United World Colleges. Since this weekend is costing you quite a lot of money, be it in dollars or pounds, I feel it is incumbent upon myself to give you a grasp of at least the barest facts about our foundation."

His voice was touched with emotion as he proceeded to tell about his uncle's deep concerns. "Shortly before his death, my uncle asked me to take on the United World Colleges as my special project, and so I have, with increasing enthusiasm and realization of the importance of training young people in how to get along with those who are culturally, racially, and ethnically not the same."

The crowd listened carefully as the prince concluded his

remarks by saying, "Now you know where your money is going and why, so maybe you would like to give just a little bit more! It's good for the soul."

Before Prince Charles called upon Armand Hammer, the American philanthropist and art collector who had so generously endowed the United World College of the American West, the prince said he had a very special announcement to make.

"The American College of the West, I am pleased to tell all of you first," said Prince Charles, "will be named for the man who has given both his time and his money to make it possible—Dr. Armand Hammer."

As Dr. Hammer came forward, there was a huge burst of applause. Despite his reputation as a crusty, hard-nosed businessman, the United World College Schools and the Prince of Wales obviously had touched a soft spot in his heart. (Several years ago Dr. Hammer donated a million dollars to the United World Colleges to found a branch in America. The money was used to purchase the site and buildings for the new college on the Gallinas River in Montezuma, New Mexico. Two days before Prince Charles' wedding, Dr. Hammer handed the deed to the Prince.)

There were murmurs of approval as Dr. Hammer announced he was adding another $8 million to his original gift, so that the existing building could be renovated and new facilities built.

Next, Lord Romsey came forward to call upon "one of the ladies who made this evening possible, Mrs. Helen Boehm from America. She has a presentation to make to Her Royal Highness, Princess Diana."

I was shocked. I had not been told I would have to speak. I thought I was going to present a sculpture privately. Well, the Franzolins had always taught their children not to delay but to go when the signal comes. I had just been given a signal! I walked in a daze toward Lord Romsey and the microphone.

"Your Royal Highness, m'lords, ladies and gentlemen, I want to thank all of you for coming such a long distance. This is a memorable evening for all of us. Thank you, all of you, for helping us raise money for such a wonderful and truly worthwhile cause."

Turning to a smiling Princess Diana, I continued, "As you

know, my company creates porcelain here in England at Malvern and, of course, in the United States at Trenton, New Jersey.

"It was our honour to have designed and created with my artisans this sculpture of the Lord Mountbatten yellow rose with the anchor and rope. We chose this particular theme not only because the Lord Mountbatten rose was selected as Rose of the Year by the Royal Rose Society in 1982, but also because Lord Mountbatten was the first Sea Lord for the British Navy and because you, Your Highness, included the Lord Mountbatten rose as one of the flowers in your wedding bouquet. And you also placed your wedding bouquet at his grave site. Because of all these meaningful facts, we have created this sculpture especially for you.

"We present it to you with much love and affection."

The tent was still (a friend later told me he could practically hear my heart beating from where he sat). Then, as the princess came forward and shyly accepted the sculpture, the guests burst into an enthusiastic round of applause. I felt such an affection for the young woman that I wanted to joke with her and whisper, "Look, I'm sorry it is just the yellow rose and not my emerald ring," but of course I couldn't summon *that* much nerve.

With the dry wit so characteristic of the English, Lord Romsey thanked everyone for coming and "for leaving behind your dollars in the United Kingdom."

"And just to give you further practice in giving," he quipped, "we are going to have a short auction to benefit the United World Colleges."

He turned the microphone over to the head of Christie's, who began the bidding for the only existing replica of the Cardinal Wolsey beaker, which I had donated. Dated 1496, this silver and gold cup with Lord Mountbatten's coat of arms on the front is decorated with lions, crowns, feathers, helmets, and shields. The original belonged to Cardinal Wolsey, Lord Chancellor during the first two years of Henry VIII's reign.

The bidding started modestly at $5,000, but as the auctioneer's assistant displayed the cup before the audience, the bidding quickly rose to $8,000, then to $12,000, and finally peaked at $50,000!

The Gucci diamond necklace and other luxuries were then

auctioned off. The bidders went really wild over a luxurious custome-made Jaguar. When the last bang of the gavel was heard, the United World College Schools were richer by $126,000.

I returned to the London airport that night in a friend's helicopter. From there I went to my hotel, accompanied by a police escort arranged by considerate British friends. I had done my best for Lord Mountbatten's cause. I was bone tired but elated, too. I was on an incredible high. Call it success.

The wakeup calls on Sunday morning came entirely too early for most people. The Thomas Amorys of New York admitted to being "just a little weary." Edwina and Emmett Barnes of Macon, Georgia, thought it was inhuman to rise so early. The Thomas Blakes of Houston "barely had time for a cup of coffee." One gentleman confessed he had overslept and didn't have time to shower—"But at least I've got on clean clothes and a liberal sprinkling of cologne."

After only four or five hours of sleep, the hearty polo enthusi- asts gathered again at the Dorchester Hotel to ride to Smith's Lawn at Windsor, not far from the great castle. Rumors floated about our coaches that the queen would be there, but they were quickly discounted by those "in the know."

Our Malvern studio director had made arrangements for a large tent adjacent to the polo field, where my American polo partner, Bill Ylvisaker, and I would entertain four hundred guests at lunch. Everyone assembled at the stroke of noon for their Pimms Cup, followed by a grand buffet. Just before the traditional dessert of delicious strawberries and thick English cream, there was a stir at the far end of the tent. It was Prince Charles. He had come to say hello and to wish me and my team good luck.

Holding a mug of ale and looking very natty in white slacks and a blue blazer, he was in great form and chatted amiably with several of our guests. "I well remember the hospital I stayed in at Palm Beach," joked the prince, referring to a heat stroke he'd suffered during a game, "and remember particularly its high bill. I certainly must get insurance before I go back."

He obviously was very much at ease with Americans. He stayed awhile at the luncheon before changing into polo clothes for the afternoon match. He, too, was playing, but not against the Boehm Team. Before leaving, he spoke to Nancy Dunnan, who told him of this book. He smilingly said, "I could tell you a few more stories about Helen Boehm."

In the meantime, many of the socialites began to parade in front of the polo club, much as at Ascot. Newspaper photographers and columnists had by this time gotten wind of the number of well-known people participating in the Polo Weekend, and the cameramen were kept busy until the start of the game. Beautiful young women with large hats attracted the most attention as they paraded on the arms of distinguished men. Margaret, Duchess of Argyll, Laurel Manenti, and Suzanne Rothschild, were favorites. John Loeb, Jr. (U.S. ambassador to Denmark at the time), was there, as well as Koo Stark, Jonathan David, and one of New York's favorite couples, John and Fifi Schiff.

At 2:30 everyone prepared to go to the stands to watch the first match, in which Prince Charles's team, Les Diables Bleus, was playing. But just before the game started, the announcer told the crowd that they must stand clear of the ropes around the polo house because "Her Majesty Queen Elizabeth will soon be here with us to dedicate the new Queen's Enclosure." (The royal family and their friends traditionally view the games from the enclosure.) The crowd was excited. The Americans were thrilled. Cameras came out of pockets and purses. People jockeyed for a better position from which to catch a glimpse of the queen. Parents boosted children onto their shoulders.

I had been invited by Colonel Watts, chairman of the Guards Polo Club, as the only American selected to sit in the Queen's Enclosure. I stood now in the roped-off area, anxiously awaiting Her Majesty's arrival.

Suddenly, the queen's car pulled up. It was a surprise. I had expected a chauffeur-driven limousine, not a country station wagon! The queen was wearing a two-piece print dress and sensible shoes. We greeted one another with warm smiles. The queen then walked to the pavilion, where she cut the white satin ribbon of her new enclosure.

Princess Di attended the match as well, sitting upstairs in the pavilion with her mother-in-law. I sat with the special polo executive committee just below the queen and the princess. After the game, the princess walked over to her own car, moved in on the driver's side, and, smiling at the surprised crowd, drove to the far side of the field to meet her polo-playing husband, who had just won his first game in the Queen's Cup match.

The excitement was not over, for the Boehm Team was on next, and the Prince and Princess of Wales stayed to watch the match. Boehm was playing Cowdray Park (Cowdray won the Queen's Cup in 1981) in the first round of the Dunhill-sponsored Queen's Cup. A long, tough game ensued, and often it seemed certain that the Boehms would lose.

The game went into overtime, with the American fans on their feet. I could barely sit still. Of course, I never gave up on my players and kept shouting encouragement to them from my position in the Queen's Enclosure, a place where one seldom hears a comment.

Of course, my boys *had* to win—and they did.

The events of the weekend did not end with one polo match. The next day the group lunched with Sir Raymond and Lady Brown at their estate in Whitley Park, and lunch was followed by polo at Cowdray Park. After that match, John Brogan gave a tea for everyone under a large tent on the polo grounds. Although Viscount Cowdray wasn't too keen on the fact that my polo team had vanquished his, he nevertheless asked me to present the trophy to the winner of the Sunday match, which I did with a great deal of satisfaction.

Following the presentation, John Brogan asked everyone to join him in thanking me, "the lady who was responsible for this Polo Weekend."

My reply was brief; then I asked those assembled for the final event of the weekend if they wanted to do it again the next year. The standing ovation and cheers told it all.

It is now an institution, an annual event that grows in numbers and in money for the charity every year. One sees some of the old faces and many new ones each year. The presence of the royals, of course, is a steadfast unchanging focus.

My love for England will always be a part of me, I guess, and it is manifested in many ways, including a step I took in July of

1983. Boehm purchased a forlorn-looking foundry in Llandow, in the heart of the industrial section of South Wales. It is one of the most depressed areas in the British Isles, and when I told Prince Charles of my acquisition, he gave a large smile and told me that the creation of new jobs would mean much to the region.

We were determined to make this Boehm foundry a success. We are now producing exquisite objects in porcelain combined with bronze as well as silver and gold. We are creating a new dimension in art forms for Boehm. Our employees are mostly relatives of unemployed coal mine workers; their willingness to work hard and with enthusiasm has been an inspiration to all of us. They are producing objects of great beauty in an area where beauty is at a premium.

The Princess of Wales, in her role as president of the Welsh Crafts Council, is interested in what we are trying to do at the foundry, and it is a nice feeling to play an active role in an Anglo-American project of such importance to art and to human lives.

38

It's Still a Forward March

I often feel like Janus, the two-headed mythological Roman figure who looks forward and backward at the same time. The pleasure in writing this book has come from looking back on what has been an unusual life, but the constant flow of energy that propels me forward keeps me looking ahead at the same time. I have many, many things to do yet in the next two or three decades.

I am convinced that many people are born with energy, drive, and optimism, but only some of them pick up the ball and run with it. Anyone who says success is easy to achieve has his head buried in the sand. There is luck—and then there is WORK! Whoever sees that the sweat of hard work and a dogged refusal to be stopped brings enormous happiness and satisfaction has 20-20 vision. (I should know; I was an optician!)

I was born into a family poor in money but very rich in love and happiness. That put me on the first Olympic team, I guess. Then I was blessed by being allowed to share twenty-five years of life with a man of great genius and depth. I was taking my path ahead when the women's movement burst into full flower, but I really was not aware of what that was all about at the time.

Today I look around me at the progress women have made and feel immense pride in understanding what we have gone through to achieve that success. I myself never felt discriminated against because of my sex, only because of an empty wallet. I never had the education of women I see entering the corporate world today, armed with college degrees and MBAs. I only hope that somewhere in those golden educations of theirs they have learned how to buckle down and work and to keep in the starting position of a runner, so they will always be ready for a clean start.

I have been told by chief executive officers of companies with whom I do business or on whose boards I have sat as a director that I am tough and demanding on matters regarding performance and holding down costs. That is praise I have earned through long experience. I also learned how to take risks when I was in grade school. It is difficult for me to understand all the rhetoric that pours out of business schools today. They say, "You *have* to learn how to take risks" as if that were something new. Of course you do. All of life is a collection of risks! And you have to work to win, then if you lose, work to win again. Entrepreneurship is the most exhausting and the most satisfying kind of activity there is, in my opinion.

Today there is still much hard work to be done. I have to help our company stay on top of the market. All of the time I am traveling around the United States and abroad, I am watching, observing, studying the market. Our company must continue to grow, and that means finding new products and new forms of art with which to please Boehm collectors and customers. When you achieve success in business, you don't just float at the top. You fight *to stay* at the top.

The great thing about my entire life story is that I have been incredibly happy through all of it, including the tough years. I'm still praying as I go, trying to pay off my debt to the Creator, who has always been there. Whatever comes along that is glorious and wonderful I'll always grab and enjoy. When I can no longer jump on an Arab steed in the desert in the moonlight, I'll find other things to do.

I think the real reason I wanted to write this book is to express a belief that regardless of where you come from, how you were raised, where you went to school, whom you marry, or how you look, what you achieve is all really up to you and your will to win.

Appendix I:
Porcelain and Its Origins in China

by Frank Cosentino,
President of Edward Marshall Boehm, Inc.

Porcelain, Earthenware, and Stoneware

From the time Marco Polo first brought back examples of fine porcelain from China in the late thirteenth century, the West has admired the medium of porcelain. Fortunes—not to mention lives—were spent in the pursuit of its secret ingredients and the mysterious formula for its creation. Western countries had already developed fine stonewares and earthenwares, but no one had mastered the technique of raising kiln temperatures to the required level; nor had anyone assembled the proper ingredients to form a translucent, vitrified ceramic. The heavy, opaque, granular Western wares did not compare to the brilliantly white, thin, light Chinese Porcelain.

As pieces of fine porcelain were brought to the West, at first in very limited numbers, monarchs of the fourteenth to seventeenth centuries vied with each other in attempts to assemble collections that would become an important measure of their wealth and prestige. At the same time, they set their chemists and alchemists to work in an attempt to duplicate the Chinese formula. It took centuries—until the year 1708 in Saxony, under the reign of Augustus the Strong—before they were able to master the technique.

The Chinese, by contrast, have a long and distinguished history in fine ceramics. As early as 6500 B.C., they were making fine earthenware pots and other utilitarian vessels from the brown clays of river banks, examples of which are in the museums of China. One can see the fingermarks of men and women from several thousand years ago who formed the pots before placing them in open fires to bake.

A largely unbroken dedication to the arts through the many Chinese dynasties allowed porcelain to evolve to the highest possible state. The Chinese have a long-held reverence for the medium, almost a religious feeling about the miracle of a fragile object in clay transformed into a hard, pearl-like object. They admired the beautiful shapes created by the ceramic artists; they were sensitive, too, to the aberrations and irregularities caused by human hands molding the humble material.

There are three basic ceramic groups—earthenware, stoneware, and porcelain. *Earthenware* is a low-fired, opaque "body" generally not exposed to temperatures in excess of 1250 degrees Fahrenheit, the melting point of glass. The fired result is a porous ceramic that does not have the strength and hardness of the higher fired media. Colors are quickly absorbed; subjects must be cast thick because of their vulnerability; glazing is essential to knit and seal the body for utilitarian use; and there is no translucence. Common earthenware names are delftware, creamware, majolica, faience, and terracotta. All are basically low-fired bodies covered over with glazes of color.

Stoneware is an earthenware formula to which flint has been added for whiteness and hardness. To fuse this composition requires temperature levels in the range of 2000 degrees Fahrenheit. The result is a fine-grained, durable ceramic with great strength that is light in color and not as weighty as earthenware. It is slightly vitrified but, like earthenware, is not translucent because no translucence-giving materials have been added to the clays. This me-

dium was refined in Europe and England during the seventeenth and eighteenth centuries. Many studios worked
with it, especially in the Staffordshire, England, production
center, where creamware, jasperware, basaltware, and
other variations were made. Today Wedgwood continues to
be a prime maker of stoneware.

The *porcelain* group is fired at temperatures up to approximately 2400 degrees Fahrenheit. The finest, whitest
kaolins are selected, milled, purified, and mixed with
feldspar and silica. Feldspar provides the "flesh" of porcelain, the binding substance that melts at high temperature
and binds the clays, or "skeletal" ingredients, into a solid,
vitrified mass. Feldspar also is responsible for the translucent qualities.

A process exclusive to the creation of porcelain takes
place when the material changes from a granular to a
molten state in the kiln. A fifteen to twenty percent
shrinkage occurs from the unfired "greenware" to the fired
porcelain, a technical and artistic consideration of prime
importance.

This feldspathic porcelain, also called "hard-paste" or
"true" porcelain, evolved in China and is still made there,
as well as in many Continental studios. Variations in the
formula—which are then known as "soft-paste"—have
been achieved in recent centuries, the most important of
which is the addition to the clays of bone ash. White
calcined (kiln dried) oxen bones are pulverized and mixed
in a proportion of 51 percent bone to 49 percent clays, and
the result is beautiful, white bone china. The English were
the first to perfect this body in the latter half of the
eighteenth century, and they continue to be recognized for
their complete mastery of it.

Other kinds of soft-paste porcelain can be made that
require less care, temperature, refinement. Bone china is
fired at about 2130 degrees Fahrenheit. A very soft body
can be made by mixing glass with the clays and reducing
the firing to 1250 degrees Fahrenheit. Vitreous materials
that can be employed include alabaster, steatite, chalk, and
modern compounds. But none is as effective or as beautiful

as bone china. Bone withstands high kiln temperatures and has excellent plasticity. It imparts the clearest translucence and whiteness of a quality to rival the finest of hard-paste porcelains; and it is the most receptive to high-fired colors.

The Boehm studio in Trenton works primarily with the hard-paste formula originally developed by Edward Boehm. To a lesser extent, Boehm is working with bone china developed by the Boehm studio in Malvern, England. Their work, of course, is heavily weighted toward bone china, although they are equally comfortable with the American hard-paste formula. The company therefore enjoys the best of both countries' traditions.

Colors and textures of ceramics can vary widely. Those not covered with glazes or enamels are called either "white bisque" or "decorated bisque," for which the Boehm studio in Trenton is well known. The Chinese developed a white bisque known as "Blanc de Chine" (which also was made with a glaze finish); English craftsmen developed a soft-paste, marblelike composition called "parian."

Glaze is a glasslike coating that renders a body impervious to liquids and stains. There are high-fired glazes that are applied over the greenware and fired once to fuse the glaze with the porcelain. Low-fired glazes are applied over the once-fired bisque, which is then fired a second time. The result, as in the case of bone china, is a layer of glaze, much like the icing on a cake, that sits on the porcelain surface. Enamels are low-fired glazes to which metallic oxides have been added.

Colors may be directly applied on greenware before glazing and the first fire, a process called "underglaze decoration." If a piece is colored after it has been glazed, then fired again, the technique is "overglaze decoration." The pigments are pure oxides—tin for opaque whites and pinks; iron for yellows and browns; iron or uranium for oranges; copper or chrome for greens; cobalt for blues; manganese or gold for purples and maroons; iron, selenium, or cadmium for reds; and a combination of iron and manganese for blacks.

The Origins of Porcelain in China

The precursor of true hard-paste porcelain, a vitrified stoneware, was developed some time during the Han Dynasty (206 B.C.–220 A.D.). It came about primarily because of progress in kiln-making, when closed, adobe-type kilns were built and fired by charcoal. Previously the kilns were open and wood-fired. It was during the Han period that the Chinese perfected one of the most beautiful palette of colors ever achieved in ceramics—celadon, a range of deep, soft greens from olive to light blue-green. Celadon resulted from glazes rich in iron fired in closed kilns.

The true porcelain formula was discovered during the Sui Dynasty (589–618 A.D.). Kilns had evolved to the point where temperatures could be raised to 2400 degrees Fahrenheit. This was due to air-tight kilns that were fired on the principle of a pressure cooker, the temperature continually rising as the fires of coal were stoked over periods of days and sometimes weeks. The palette had by now expanded into copper greens and reds.

The Tang Dynasty (618–907 A.D.) was a period of accelerating change in Chinese ceramics. Thinner, purer glazes and more refined bodies were mastered. Pottery and stoneware kept pace with porcelain and now were covered with three-color lead glazes. Some blues, yellow oranges, new greens, and cream glazes appeared. The dynasty saw increasing commercial activity between China and her neighbors, India, the Middle East, Persia, Japan, and Korea. Merchants were eager to visit the "land of silk." They came by sea from Egypt; the Slavs came by land over the long and treacherous Tartary Road. The influx of foreign ideas and images provided creative stimuli to China and its arts. For example, Tang horses, the subjects in ceramics most associated with the period, were inspired by Iranian and Arabian horsemen who came to play polo for the pleasure of the Chinese emperors.

In the Sung Dynasty (960–1280), kiln sophistication increased. In the Foshan ceramic center, located on the outskirts of Canton, there exists a kiln that is more than one hundred feet long and pitched on a thirty-degree hill. It really is a series of cavelike kilns, one above the other, with periodic landings for loading and unloading. The chambers are divided into high-fire and low-fire zones, and as many as ten thousand pieces can be fired simultaneously. The longest and largest "flat" tunnel kiln in operation today in China is in the Wei Min factory of Ching-te-Chen, with a capacity more than double the one in Foshan.

During the Sung period, glazes took on greater variety, additional colors were formulated, and more experimentation was employed in decorating techniques. Colors were mixed together into glazes; separate color glazes were applied over one another, then carved through to reveal two or more layers; crackled glaze was created by mismatching a high-fire body with a low-fire glaze, then force cooling. The dominant colors were celadon, black, brown, white, buff, green, and blue.

One of the bleakest periods in China's history was the Yuan Dynasty (1280–1368), when the feared Genghis Khan, and later his grandson, Kublai Khan, overran the country. This was the period when Marco Polo traveled from Venice, arriving in 1274 and staying for a visit that was to last seventeen years. There was little progress in the arts under the Mongols, although porcelain making did continue on a reduced scale. Much of what was made was white, the reason Marco Polo called the medium "porcellana," after a white seashell named "genus *porcellana.*" Some new additions were seen in color refinement and styles of decoration. Incised sgraffito, carved and molded relief designs, and design appliqués began to appear.

When the Chinese drove out the Mongols, it marked the beginning of a great new period. The Ming Dynasty (1368–1644) was a time of flourishing commercial activity with the West and the rest of the world; an intellectual and cultural resurgence took place simultaneously with the Renaissance in Europe. The arts flourished—lacquer work, bronze sculpture, cloisonné, jade and ivory carvings—spurred by foreign demand and influence.

Like their predecessors, the early Ming emperors preferred subtle monochrome decoration. They considered it a sacrilege to cover so beautiful and respected a medium with too much decoration. Polychrome gradually became fashionable, however, particularly under Western influence. The combination of blue and white became popular first, then other two-color pairings, and eventually five-color combinations of red, yellow, green, blue, violet. Other decorative schemes included white-ware with "hidden decoration" (subtle modeling on the white surface); polychromes in layered relief; open and cutout cloisonné techniques; reserve decoration (leaving incised designs unglazed for later enameling); contrasting color (a magnificent technique of underglaze blue and white with overglaze enamels); and the introduction of pure gold and gold leaf.

It was during the Ming period that Ching-te-Chen became the imperial production center, and twenty-five thousand workers still produce the country's finest porcelain there today. Ching-te-Chen specializes in handcrafting and handpainting of fine tablewares, tea and coffee sets, vases and urns of all sizes, trays, and porcelain paintings. The finest Chinese porcelain body of all—the lightbulb-thin, almost transparent "eggshell porcelain"—is made here.

The end of the Ming period was a disruptive era in Chinese history, and struggles for power led to several decades of war. Finally, the Manchus took control and established the important Ching Dynasty in 1644. It was to last until 1911. Ching-te-Chen, which had been destroyed, was rebuilt, and the world's greatest period of fine ceramic production began, stimulated by the great Western trading companies.

As the West rediscovered the secret formula and started to build its own porcelain centers, the craving for Chinese exports declined. The last of the great Ching periods was the Chien Lung from 1736 to 1796, after which the techniques, materials, and knowledge spread throughout the world, one production center merging with the other or borrowing and copying styles and designs. But in spite of the paucity of great work from China in recent decades and all that has been lost through centuries of pilferage, destruction, and plagiarism, the world has been enriched by China's enormous contributions to the knowledge and appreciation of fine porcelain.

Appendix II:
Boehm Porcelain
Represented Internationally

(Museums, hospitals, universities, schools, palaces, and other prominent places)

The White House, Washington, D.C.
Buckingham Palace, London, England
Elysee Palace, Paris, France
The Vatican, Rome, Italy
Peking, The People's Republic of China
Moscow
The Israel Museum, Jerusalem
The Tel Aviv Museum, Israel
Ha'Aretz Museum, Tel Aviv, Israel
Abdine Palace, Cairo, Egypt
Smithsonian Institution, Washington, D.C.
John F. Kennedy Center, Washington, D.C.
The Metropolitan Museum of Art, New York
Bellingrath Gardens, Mobile, Alabama
Royal Ontario Museum, Toronto, Canada
Kyung Mu Dai, Seoul, Korea
Royal Palace, Stockholm, Sweden
Liverpool Museum, England
Royal Palace, Monaco

City Museum and Art Gallery, Stoke-on-Trent, England
City Museum, Worcester, England
Tokyo National Museum, Japan
American Embassy, London, England
American Embassy, Copenhagen, Denmark
American Embassy, Rothschild Mansion, Paris, France
New Jersey State Museum, Trenton
Los Angeles County Museum, California
Houston Museum of Fine Arts, Texas
Brooks Memorial Art Gallery, Memphis, Tennessee
Louisiana State Museum, New Orleans
Birmingham Museum of Art, Alabama
Louisiana Arts & Science Center, Baton Rouge
Arkansas Arts Center, Little Rock
Dallas Museum of Natural History, Texas
Indianapolis Museum of Art, Indiana
Lyndon Baines Johnson Library, Austin, Texas

212

Syracuse University Museum, New York

Wichita Art Museum, Kansas

Governor's Mansion, Raleigh, North Carolina

Washington County Museum, Hagerstown, Maryland

North Carolina Museum of Art, Raleigh

Fine Arts Gallery, San Diego, California

Heritage Plantation of Sandwich, Massachusetts

Liberty Village, Flemington, New Jersey

Houston Museum of Natural Science, Texas

American Camellia Society, Fort Valley, Georgia

Truman Library, Independence, Missouri

Blair House, Washington, D.C.

The University of Texas, San Antonio

Cummer Gallery of Art, Jacksonville, Florida

Louisiana State University, Baton Rouge

Missouri Botanical Garden, St. Louis

State Historical Museum, Jackson, Mississippi

The Birks Museum, Millikin University, Decatur, Illinois

University of Richmond, Virginia

Mayo Clinic, Rochester, Minnesota

University of North Florida, Jacksonville

LaGrange College, Georgia

Newark Museum, New Jersey

John R. and Eleanor R. Mitchell Foundation, Mt. Vernon, Illinois

Henry Ford Museum, Dearborn, Michigan

Concordia College, River Forest, Illinois

Huggins Hospital, Wolfeboro, New Hampshire

The Hun School, Princeton, New Jersey

The Evansville Museum of Arts & Sciences, Indiana

Central National Bank, San Angelo, Texas

Scheie Eye Institute, Philadelphia, Pennsylvania

Buffalo Museum of Science, New York

Fort Smith Art Center, Arkansas

Museum of New Mexico, Santa Fe

Museum of Science & Space Transit Planetarium, Miami, Florida

Children's Hospital, New Orleans, Louisiana

Danville Museum, Virginia

Florida House, Washington, D.C.

The Butler Institute of American Art, Youngstown, Ohio

College of Notre Dame, Baltimore, Maryland

Fairhope Public Library, Alabama

The Fine Arts Museum of the South at Mobile, Alabama

Memorial Art Gallery, Rochester, New York

Drexel University, Philadelphia, Pennsylvania

El Paso Museum of Art, Texas

St. Jude Children's Hospital, Memphis, Tennessee

Crippled Children's Hospital, Memphis, Tennessee

Chicago Horticultural Society Botanic Gardens, Illinois

Jacksonville Children's Hospital, Florida

Jacksonville Museum of Arts and Sciences, Florida

Terrebonne Historical and Cultural Society, Houma, Louisiana

Pennsylvania State University, Altoona

Saint Lawrence Rehabilitation Center, Lawrenceville, New Jersey

St. Peter's College, Jersey City, New Jersey

The Museum of Arts and Sciences, Daytona Beach, Florida

Mobile City Museum, Alabama

The Virginia Museum of Fine Arts, Richmond

St. John Medical Center, Tulsa, Oklahoma

The Oklahoma Museum of Art,
Oklahoma City
Delaware Technical and Community
College Museum, Georgetown
Gulf Coast Art Association, Biloxi,
Mississippi
Tampa Museum, Florida
Trenton City Museum, New Jersey
Audubon Wildlife Sanctuary,
Audubon, Pennsylvania
Rahr-West Museum, Manitowoc,
Wisconsin
Henry B. Plant Museum, Tampa,
Florida
Jessie C. Wilson Art Galleries,
Anderson College, Indiana
McDonogh School, Maryland
University of Osteopathic Medicine &
Health Sciences, Des Moines,
Iowa

Our Lady of the Lakes Regional
Medical Center, Baton Rouge,
Louisiana
The Methodist Hospital in Houston,
Texas
Wichita Art Association, Inc.,
Wichita, Kansas
Stark Museum of Art, Orange, Texas
Carson County Square House
Museum, Panhandle, Texas
The University of Utah, Salt Lake
City
Capital Children's Museum,
Washington, D.C.
Nyack Hospital, New York
Historical Society of Rockland
County, New City, New York
Buffalo Zoological Gardens, New York

Index